INTOXICATED
WITH
BABYLON

THE SEDUCTION OF GOD'S PEOPLE IN THE LAST DAYS

STEVE GALLAGHER

INTOXICATED WITH BABYLON

THE SEDUCTION OF GOD'S PEOPLE IN THE LAST DAYS

Comments About
Intoxicated with Babylon

"Another outstanding book by Steve Gallagher!"
THE WRITER'S EDGE
Book Reviewers

"*Intoxicated with Babylon* is an urgent message for the church today. Steve's careful presentation of the origin and history of the world system helps the believer to understand its deception and power to lure. God's call to His Church reverberates throughout the book—a call to holiness without being lured by the world's glamour or tainted by its spirit. Few books are written with such clarity and depth concerning the call to God's people to be freed from the world system and to walk with Him. This book has challenged me and I know it will challenge the reader."
DR. RUTH RUIBAL
Missionary, Cali, Colombia

"Steve Gallagher has emerged in our day as a strong voice that God is using to help people get free and stay free from the lusts of this world. Steve Gallagher serves as an oracle of the Lord calling again to God's people to come out and be a separate and holy people. This word could not have come at a timelier hour. Could it be that America is ready to repent? Could it be that America is ripe for harvest? Could it be that the world is ripe for harvest? May God use this as a handbook to help the saint and sinner get free and stay free so we can serve God in a true spirit of holiness!!"
REV. JOHN KILPATRICK
Pensacola, FL

"*Intoxicated with Babylon* is a call to each of us, and to the Evangelical Church. It is a 'wake-up call'... a very loud one that cannot be ignored. You will either respond and get out of 'bed' immediately, or you will hit the 'snooze button' and go back to sleep. It is a clear choice leading to the opportunity for repentance and serious faith in Christ. Those who hit the 'snooze button' will prove Steve Gallagher's thesis that the Church in America has drifted far from the mark. The choice is clear—sleep or awaken!

"Those who are awakened and alert to this opportunity to repent and follow Christ will want to radically examine and change how they are living their life. They will also want to share this wake-up call with others who may have also been lulled into a nap by the forces of this world. I am glad I had an opportunity to respond to the alarm."

JIM SHEARD
Author of *In His Grip*

"*Intoxicated with Babylon* is very informative for people who want to hear and see. They will be challenged to repent and make new commitments. Unfortunately, the masses will continue to walk in the darkness of deception unless God intervenes. But Steve, like Jeremiah of old, is still commanded to cry the message even though people will not always listen. I feel this book is a definite wake-up call to the Church in these last days."

REV. KENNETH KASHNER
Haverhill, MA

For books and other teaching resources please contact:

PURE LIFE MINISTRIES
14 School Street
Dry Ridge, KY 41035
(888) PURELIFE - to order
www.purelifeministries.org

ISBN/EAN 978-0-9758832-4-2
eBook ISBN/EAN 978-0-9846605-1-3

I Dedicate this Book to the Saints of God

The following quotes express my heart:

"I want to be a more serious-minded Christian man, more detached from this world, more ready for heaven than I have ever been in my whole life. I want an ear that is sharp to know the voice of the enemy, whether it comes from religion, politics, or philosophy. I want to know when I'm hearing the soft, soothing voice of Antichrist preparing me psychologically for a takeover. I would rather stand and have everybody my enemy than to go along with the crowd to destruction. Do you feel that way?"
-A.W. Tozer

"I do not set up myself to be better than other people, and if anyone asks, 'What are you, that you write this way?' I answer, 'I am a very poor creature indeed.' But I say that I cannot read the Bible without desiring to see many believers more spiritual, more holy, more single-eyed, more heavenly-minded, more whole-hearted than they (presently) are. I want to see among believers more of a pilgrim spirit, a more decided separation from the world, a conversation more evidently in heaven, a closer walk with God, and therefore I have written as I have."
- J.C. Ryle

Contents

FOREWORD

Maintaining a 'love affair with the world' is akin to having a mistress. In many of today's cultures, keeping a mistress is an acceptable practice, providing some excitement to an otherwise boring life and marriage.

The modern-day Church, especially in the West, has its own mistress, having fallen head-over-heels in love with the world. The average believer can talk for hours about 'the things of the world' but then try asking about their relationship with the Lord and they quickly run out of words. The Bible says 'out of the abundance of the heart the mouth speaks.'

When a person is in love, they will enthusiastically tell you all about their lover. Paul warned us that in the last days, men would be lovers of money, lovers of pleasure, lovers of self more than lovers of God. These are some of the 'lovers' that creep into our lives and gradually erode our relationship with God. Jesus said in the last days the 'love of many would wax cold.' How well this describes the condition of the present-day Church. Over time, the Church's passion for Christ has cooled from its former fervency and fire to what is now only a smoldering ember.

James refers to those who love the world as adulterers. Tragically, the vast majority of Christians are even now pursuing an ongoing love affair with the world. Every Sunday they convey a false image to others that their marriage to Christ is impeccable, yet in reality they derive far more excitement from their interaction with the world. The spirit of this world is a powerful and cunning seductress that few seem able to discern and from whom even fewer seem able to disengage themselves. She craftily flatters with her lips, deceiving people into a false sense of security while they partake of her enticements. But as the book of Proverbs says "many are the victims she has cast down and numerous are all her slain. Her house is the way to Sheol." (Proverbs 7:25-27)

Imagine what it would be like on your wedding day to hear your spouse say these words: "I _____ take you _____ to be my lawfully wedded_____. I promise to remain faithful to you on Sundays only. I refuse to forsake all former lovers, choosing rather to cling to them and meet with them throughout the week." No one in their right mind would agree to such an arrangement! And yet, that is exactly how many Christians treat the Lord—our Heavenly Bridegroom.

Steve Gallagher spares no punches in this book as he seeks to expose and destroy this 'worldly' mistress. You will appreciate the masterful and insightful way that he deals with this subject. Gallagher's desire is to see the Church restored to her first love—Christ Himself.

If the passion is missing from your relationship with Jesus Christ, then this book is for you. Read it honestly, prayerfully and frequently, asking the Holy Spirit to remove the blindness and calloused indifference from your life. Then ask Him to grant you that gracious gift of repentance that results in restored fellowship and intimacy with the Lover of your soul.

DAVID RAVENHILL

Author, Itinerant Teacher—Siloam Springs, Arkansas

INTRODUCTION

Babylon is the power of Satan at work in the hearts of mankind. This is not a new phenomenon but rather something very ancient. Its insidious efforts began in the Garden of Eden, when the serpent—with monstrous subtlety—convinced Eve that the *mixed* knowledge of good and evil would put her on par with God. The moment her lips touched that forbidden fruit, her soul was polluted, her mind darkened and she came under the dreadful power of sin and death. The primeval couple discovered that they had crossed a terrible boundary and left an existence they could never reclaim. "Man's mind," Oliver Wendell Holmes wrote, "once stretched by a new idea never regains its original dimension."

Over the next two or three thousand years, the corruption of mankind deepened until "every intent of the thoughts of (man's) heart was only evil continually." (Genesis 6:5) Then, after repeated warnings from Noah, the massive Flood overwhelmed and buried mankind in a vast, worldwide ocean of judgment.

The Lord started over again with one family. But the germinating seed of corruption remained within man's breast. The ember of lust continued to smolder in men's hearts, waiting for just the right evil wind to fan new life into it. Within four generations, it came, when an insurrection against Jehovah broke out in the fertile plains of Mesopotamia. The tower and city of Babel were created as a new alternative to what they considered to be the dreary worship of Jehovah—Lord of the Semites.

It was there, in Babylon, that the forces of darkness gained new momentum in their war on God. In ancient Babylon, Lucifer's rebellion now became *systematized*. No longer would the enemy's efforts be confined to the enticement of individuals towards sin. Satan had established a "national" mindset, unifying men in their rebellion against God's law. Its value system was based on a person's temporal, rather than eternal, good. Since man was created with a conscience and an inherent need to feel that he is doing "right," the enemy quietly formed his own unspoken set of guidelines which determined the acceptability of man's behavior. All of this was done as an alternative to the standards, values and perspectives of God's Kingdom.

This universal mindset can be traced down through the ages to modern times and is still alive and thriving amongst us today.

The "world" is Satan's unified system which lies outside the Kingdom of God. This would not be so dangerous to God's people if it were openly presented as an obvious alternative to what the Lord has established amongst believers—those people who are adherents to His Kingdom. The peril lies in the subtlety of the powers at work within the Church and within our individual lives. Like a cancer, the spirit of the world quietly, steadily and methodically attacks one cell at a time, infiltrating our churches, our families and our lives and largely supplanting God's value system with a new hybrid.

Introduction

Paul worried that, "as the serpent deceived Eve by his craftiness, your minds will be led astray from the simplicity and purity of devotion to Christ." (1 Corinthians 10:21) It is the simple (not mixed) and the pure (not polluted) devotion to Christ that believers are called to live.

Scripture is very straightforward about the need for consecrated living. However, the majority of people can't face the thought of living without all of their worldly attractions, convincing themselves that living with *mixture* is acceptable to the Lord.

People are only vulnerable to being deceived when they want what is being offered to them.

As man's day draws to a close and we approach the great Day of the Lord, this unseen war rages like never before. Satan's wrath is being poured out against believers. (Revelation 12:12) The spirit of Antichrist is wearing down the holy resolve of the saints. (Daniel 7:25)

Now, at this crucial hour, God's people have corporately approved of a powerless form of religion that tolerates an impotent blend of Christianity and heathenism. "They worshiped the Lord," the Bible says of idolatrous Israel, "but they also served their own gods in accordance with the customs of the nations." (2 Kings 17:33 NIV) No wonder the Lord exclaimed, "I cannot endure iniquity and the solemn assembly." (Isaiah 1:13)

In my own life, I too have had to face worldliness. The greatest source of spiritual contamination for me came from television. Every night for years, I would plop down in front of the TV and watch old reruns. Then, in early 1985, God began dealing with me about it until I finally repented and got rid of our television.

Within a year, the Lord led me to begin Pure Life Ministries. By this time, having been away from television for some time, I could better see the effect it had had on my life and was having on the lives of those to whom I was now ministering. From the very beginning of my work with sexual addicts, the evils of TV were a prominent theme in my teachings.

Then, in 1993, God put a passion in me to study the Book of Revelation. No Bible study I have ever done compares to what I undertook with this apocalyptic book. I was unprepared for how intensely this study gripped me. All total, I spent over twelve hundred hours* scrutinizing every chapter and verse of Revelation. I listened to sermons on tape, read books and studied commentaries. I prayed over the verses, one by one. I studied the Book of Revelation inductively, and listened to a dramatization of the book on cassette so many times I wore out the tape.

Studying this tremendous book literally became a full-time job—I typically spent forty hours a week in this study. God used the riches I found in the *Pulpit Commentary* and commentaries written by old-time saints such as Adam Clarke, Matthew Henry, John Wesley and others to instill a driving hunger for truth in my heart.

At times, the realities of the spiritual realm—where the mighty conflict exists between the Kingdom of Light and the kingdom of darkness—actually became more real to me than the world around me. The message I uncovered in that Bible study affected me very deeply, altering the entire course of my life. I struggle at times but continue to respond to His call: a call that sounds forth to all Christendom.

A 2018 UPDATE

Over the years since I wrote the original version of this book, I have received many, many letters and emails by people who have had some of the same revelations about the Last

---

* I probably spent another 3,000 hours going back through the book of Revelation after that period in 1993.

Days that I penned. For instance, I was recently contacted by Steve Harrison who wrote a book in 2011 entitled, *The Clash of Kingdoms: Rediscovering Our Role in Earth's Greatest Battle.* He had not read *Intoxicated with Babylon* when he wrote his book. Nevertheless, he had many of the same revelations I had regarding the Last Days. With his kind permission, I have shared a number of them throughout this new revision. The following is one such example:

> I believe Babylon is actually a belief system based on the premise, "We do not need God." Babylon represents fallen humanity's desperate effort to establish its own universal value system. It is the kingdom of man independent of God. This kingdom seeks happiness and meaning without God's involvement. It is determined to reach its goals and develop its future without His leadership. Its citizens are not extreme atheists but common people whose lifestyles reflect an independence from the God of the Bible. Ironically, according to a recent poll, 92 percent of Americans believe in God, so belief is not the issue. The problem is that we live as though we do not need Him![1]

Another book I have recently encountered that offers similar truths on this subject is *Worldliness: Resisting the Seduction of a Fallen World* by C.J. Mahaney. For instance, he points out, "Today, the greatest challenge facing American evangelicals is not persecution from the world, but seduction by the world."[2] He goes on to offer his meaningful definition:

> Worldliness, then… is to gratify and exalt oneself to the exclusion of God. It rejects God's rule and replaces it with our own (like creating our own Bibles). It exalts our opinions above God's truth. It elevates our sinful desires

for the things of this fallen world above God's commands and promises.[3] (Emphasis in original.)

Unquestionably, the Lord continues to call His people to separate themselves from this fallen world system. The message remains virtually the same regardless of the vessel who shares it: "Come out of her, my people, that you may not participate in her sins and that you may not receive of her plagues; for her sins have piled up as high as heaven, and God has remembered her iniquities." (Revelation 18:4-5)

I invite you to join me in my quest for a rich life in God. For you and I will never know the treasures of heaven as long as we are *Intoxicated with Babylon.*

PART ONE

A BIBLICAL MANDATE

"I looked for the church and found it in the world.
I looked for the world and found it in the church."
-Andrew Bonar

"The heart of man is narrow, and cannot contain both loves. The world draws down the heart from God; and so the more the love of the world prevails the more the love of God dwindles and decays.... The Spirit of God in true Christians is opposed to the spirit of the world."[1]

-Matthew Henry

1

The Spirit
of the World

A rocky, barren penal colony established by the
ruthless disciplinarians of Rome was no place for a
man in his nineties. It hardly seems fair that God
would have allowed the old "apostle of love" to be banished
to a Roman labor camp and forced to work with the most
hardened criminals of the Roman Empire. But the ways of
God are often hidden to the logical mind of man. While the
Isle of Patmos was a place of unspeakable agony and suffering
for his fellow prisoners, to John it was a place where all the
luxuries and frills of this world were gloriously absent.
There was little to distract him from the Wonderful Face of
his beloved Savior. It was said by those who knew him that
in his waning years all John ever spoke of was love and that
Being of Love—such devotion is clearly expressed in his first
epistle. Captivated by the sight of Jesus, he was unruffled by
the sights and sounds of the hellish chaos around him. He
thought only of his Beloved whose Name was continually on
his lips, whose Face was etched into his memory.

But there was more to John's private life than "beatific vision." For years God had been giving him foretastes of what would occur prior to Jesus' return. John had seen glimpses of the great spiritual contest between Light and Darkness that would reach a climax at the end of this age. The theater for this apocalyptic conflict would be the planet earth, and the stage would be the hearts of mankind. "And now, little children," he had written earlier, "abide in Him, so that when He appears, we may have confidence and not shrink away from Him in shame at His coming." (1 John 2:28)

Although John had an intimation of these things, they remained hidden behind a curtain. Now the rigors of Patmos were driving John into God like never before. John was "IN the Spirit" when suddenly the thin veil that separated him from his Savior disappeared and the very door of heaven opened before his eyes. It was The Unveiling (Revelation) of Jesus Christ! As John lay at Jesus' feet depleted of all human strength, the heavens were opened, and he was shown tremendous and amazing mysteries.

The inspired truths he had recorded in his epistles were now enacted in glorious scenes right before him. He saw the glory and triumph of a Bride "without spot or wrinkle!" But he also saw the unfolding of a great demonic deception that would one day smother the earth, causing many followers of Christ to fall away from the faith.

The conflict John witnessed, which is the subject of this book, could be summed up in the words he had penned earlier:

Do not love the world, nor the things in the world. If anyone loves the world, the love of the Father is not in him. For all that is in the world, the lust of the flesh and the lust of the eyes and the boastful pride of life, is not from the Father, but is from the world. And the world is passing away, and also its lusts; but the one who does the will of God abides forever. (1 John 2:15-17)

THE SPIRIT OF THE WORLD

C.J. Mahaney offers his thoughts on John's statement:

"Do not love the world or anything in the world" (NIV).
There's nothing subtle about this sentence. It's abrupt and to the point—only ten words. It is categorical: "Do not love the world." It's comprehensive: "Do not love anything in the world." And it's intrusive, strategically aimed at whatever we desire most: "anything in the world."
It forbids worldliness in no uncertain terms.[2]

Truly, John is describing the battle which will be fought out in the hearts and minds of God's people in the last days. Those who choose to be followers of Christ will have to face hard choices.

+ Will the lust of the flesh rule their hearts?
+ Will the lust of the eyes govern their choices?
+ Will the lust for position lead them away from Jesus' feet?

In short, will they do the will of God? The Scriptures indicate that many will succumb to the delusion that they can indulge themselves in the world and its "things" and still maintain a love for the Father. How mistaken the many are!

There are three terms in this passage of Scripture which constitute the vocabulary of this great conflict. These three words—*world, lust* and *love*—are extremely important for us to consider and are worth taking a few moments to examine.

THE WORLD

As I studied this important passage of Scripture, I began to research the Greek word *kosmos*, translated by the English word "world." I found the following definition for this term buried in an old theological dictionary written back in the 1930s:

Kosmos has various senses connected with "order." It thus denotes "what is well assembled or constructed from its individual parts"....

The senses previously mentioned all merge in that of the cosmic order. The use of *kosmos* for the universe is widespread and goes back to an early period. The idea is that there is an order of things that corresponds to the order of human law. Individual things are at odds, as people engage in disputes, but an immanent cosmic norm holds things together as law does society. The world itself is thus viewed as an ordered society.[3]

The discovery of this definition got me thinking about the aspects involved in any view of "the world." At first it was difficult to imagine how there could be any order in our chaotic world of seven and a half billion individual wills. Ethnic wars, conflicting philosophies, widely differing languages, competing lusts for power, position and pleasure, all hinder the human race from being in agreement on much of anything.

Shortly after that, I ran across the following description of *kosmos* in *The Pulpit Commentary*, which helped me gain a better sense of what "the world" is as we know it.

(*Kosmos*) is a term specifically used by St. John to denote the ordered whole of the universe, viewed apart from God.... From being thus the scene of ordered existence apart from God, it rapidly moves into the organized resistance to the will of God, and therefore it often denotes humanity taken as a whole apart from God and grace.[4]

Supplied with this new evidence, I did a thorough study of this important concept in the Scripture, reminding myself that *kosmos* meant "an ordered existence apart from God." What became clear to me was that, although sometimes the word refers to everyone living on the planet earth (John 3:16), it is used primarily to describe the *corporate consciousness* of the people of this world who are in rebellion against God's authority. *Kosmos* is what binds together the unbelieving world. It is a global mentality that remains a powerful unspoken force in the lives of mankind. It molds vastly different people groups into one entity which lives out its existence on earth under the domain of Satan, *unified against God*.

Still later, I ran across the following comments from Watchman Nee, who brings out the dilemma God's people face:

> There is, then an ordered system, "the world," which is governed from behind the scenes by a ruler, Satan... Using this earth as his springboard and man as his tool, he usurped God's creation to make of it instead something centered in himself and reflecting his own image... So today we are confronted by two worlds, two spheres of authority, having two totally different and opposed characters... Thus salvation is not so much a personal question of sins forgiven or of hell avoided. It is to be seen rather in terms of a system from which we come out.[5]

A SCRIPTURAL HISTORY OF *KOSMOS*

My studies on this subject took me back to the beginning of creation where we are told that after God created the heavens and the earth, He "saw that it was good." (Genesis 1:31) He then made man in His own image and enjoyed unbroken fellowship with him. Even though God had given man dominion over everything in the earth, there was a great turning away from Him when Adam sinned. Something was lost that fallen man could not himself reclaim. Paul explains that, "through one man sin entered into the world." (Romans 5:12) When that happened, man relinquished ownership of this planet to the devil.

When Satan tried to tempt Jesus, he "took Him to a very high mountain, and showed Him all the kingdoms of the world, and their glory; and he said to Him, 'All these things will I give You, if You fall down and worship me.'" (Matthew 4:8-9) Jesus did not deny they were his to give. The Lord understood that this fallen angel of light owned the kingdoms of the world since the time Adam entered a partnership with him in the Garden. Satan, the founder and chief perpetrator of rebellion, is the mastermind behind the global mentality that is against God, having managed to bring almost all of mankind into his (spirit of) rebellion.

In Revelation, it is that serpent of old who will deceive the entire world. (Revelation 12:9; 13:14) Paul calls Satan "the god of this world." (2 Corinthians 4:4) Jesus refers to him as "the ruler of this world." (John 12:31; 16:11) John explains that "the whole world lies in the power of the evil one." (1 John 5:19) He also said, "This is the spirit of the Antichrist, of which you have heard that it is coming, and now it is already in the world." (1 John 4:3) While the word *kosmos* refers primarily to the people who are in this anti-God system, it also refers to the global consciousness of those people or to the spirit that controls their thinking. Thus, *the spirit of kosmos* is none other than Satan himself.

To help us have a better awareness of who we are really dealing with, I have taken a few Scriptures that refer to the devil and have substituted the phrase, *spirit of the world* in its place:

> You are of your father *the spirit of the world*, and you want to do the desires of your father. He was a murderer from the beginning, and does not stand in the truth, because there is no truth in him. Whenever he speaks a lie, he speaks from his own nature; for he is a liar, and the father of lies. But because I speak the truth, you do not believe Me. (John 8:44-45)

The Spirit of the World

Submit therefore to God. Resist *the spirit of the world* and he will flee from you. (James 4:7)

Be of sober spirit, be on the alert. Your adversary, *the spirit of the world*, prowls about like a roaring lion, seeking someone to devour. But resist him, firm in your faith. (1 Peter 5:8-9)

Little children, let no one deceive you; the one who practices righteousness is righteous, just as He is righteous; the one who practices sin is of *the spirit of the world*; for *the spirit of the world* has sinned from the beginning. The Son of God appeared for this purpose, that He might destroy the works of *the spirit of the world*. No one who is born of God practices sin, because His seed abides in him; and he cannot sin, because he is born of God. By this the children of God and the children of *the spirit of the world* are obvious: anyone who does not practice righteousness is not of God, nor the one who does not love his brother. (1 John 3:7-10)

The spirit that continually offers such intoxicating rewards is the same spirit that seeks to destroy man. The charms he uses to entice us, far from being innocuous, become avenues for him to enter the human heart.

The Lust of the World

The spirit of the world thrives wherever man pursues "the lust of the flesh and the lust of the eyes and the boastful pride of life." Anyone dominated by these ungodly passions is worldly. Devils thrive on such lusts of violence, greed and all the other passions to which humans yield themselves. I know that to be true from my own experience.

Years ago when I was still an avid TV watcher, Star Trek reruns were the highlight of many of my evenings. I remember a particular episode involving the presence of Klingons aboard the Starship Enterprise. There was an uneasy alliance between them and the crewmen of the Enterprise. Unbeknownst to all, there was also another visitor aboard the spaceship. It was an invisible being that gained its nourishment and strength through the expended energy of hatred and violence of others.

This (evil) being would create scenarios that incited battles between the two opposing groups. Whenever they fought, it would grow in strength. Captain Kirk finally figured it out, and the show ended with the Klingons and Federation members all laughing together and driving the intruder out with their camaraderie.

This is an excellent picture of the evil forces that prey upon the fleshly passions of men. For example, go into a prison, and you will almost see demons thriving and expanding themselves on the hatred and prideful competition among inmates. Visit an adult bookstore, and you will sense leering devils acting out their perversions through the bodies of men. Spend an evening in a bar, and you will witness spirits of carousing and drunkenness hypnotizing their victims into a numbing stupor. Walk through any mall, and you will see people being goaded into a buying frenzy by the latest fashions and fads. Attend many churches, and you will discern religious spirits lulling the unsuspecting into a false sense of peace with God.

The world has a thousand charms to lure the believer away from a vibrant, genuine love relationship with God. James said, "But each one is tempted when he is carried away and enticed by his own lust." (James 1:14) Every human being has within his fallen nature numerous lusts which the spirit of the world targets. A person's urge to possess or experience "the things in the world" can be so powerful that his desire for them chokes out his desire for truth. The enemy glamorizes the satisfactions which our lusts crave, leaving us to bounce from one lie to the next, constantly seeking an illusionary fulfillment that never materializes. This phenomenon is exactly what Jesus was referring to when He talked about those who allowed "the worries of the world, and the deceitfulness of riches, and the desires for other things (to) enter in and choke the word." (Mark 4:18-19)

The more a believer indulges in the lusts of the world, the more corrupted he will become inside. His love for God, which once might have burned intensely, will dissipate eventually into a mere outward façade of religious activity. He may glibly say, "I love the Lord with all my heart," yet devote his time and energy to the attractions of this present world, putting God into a secondary and minor place in his life. The spirit of the world takes direct aim at professing Christians such as this. With a life centering on the wishes and cravings of his flesh, how can he not be vulnerable to its influence?

These three carnal appetites, the lust of the flesh, the lust of the eyes, and the lust of pride, are branches of sin. The lust of the flesh represents the entire realm of pleasure, entertainment, amusement, and comfort, and includes addictions, movies, sports, television, the internet, travel, and all the many kinds of activities people become involved in. The lust of the eyes describes a person's intense desire to have something he sees. It usually revolves around the desire for possessions: trendy clothes, the latest technology, a new car, and so on. The pride of life is a person's exaggerated estimate of his own value as a person. Self-ambition, a drive to be successful, to have more prominence, an urge to "keep up with the Joneses," or the prideful desire to "be the one"—these are the evidences of the pride of life.

The entire evil tree with its three main branches could be described by the single term coveting, which in its simplest meaning is *the desire for something for self*. Most of the things mentioned above are permissible by the Lord when they are kept in their proper place. As David Powlison says, "The evil in our desires often lies not in what we want, but in the fact that we want it too much."[6]

The trouble is that Christians have allowed these lusts to drive them in much the same way the unsaved are driven. In fact, in the daily life, it is difficult to see any difference between the two.

This world caters to these passions, and the Whore of Babylon operates a house of pleasures that will give anybody—whether they call themselves Christian or not—what they want. In later chapters, we will discuss how the spirit of the world has used these lusts to make various inroads into the Church.

LOVE—A MATTER OF DEVOTION

Make no mistake about it—there is an intense battle for the heart of every single person who professes Christ as Lord. John admonished believers, "Do not love the world, nor the things in the world. If anyone loves the world, the love of the Father is not in him." This clear-cut statement describes the fierce competition which goes on for a person's devotion, for a person's heart. At any rate, he is either devoted to God or he is not, the telltale factor lying in the true interests of his life. Jesus said it this way: "For where your treasure is, there will your heart be also." (Matthew 6:21) A person's treasure is simply that which is most valuable to him, what he *loves*. Without exception, a person will be led throughout life by what he cherishes most.

The Greek word *agapao* is our English word "love." In its New Testament usage it is used primarily to describe the daily life of the true Christian. In essence, it portrays the overriding passion of a believer's soul. Jesus said, "You shall love the Lord your God with all your heart, and with all your soul, and with all your mind. This is the great and foremost commandment." (Matthew 22:37-38) In other words, everything a Christian does in life should be motivated by and controlled by a deep affection for the Lord. Anyone who is truly living in this commandment has been weaned from all competing affections. All his heart, all his soul, and all his mind are centered upon Jesus. His entire inner man is filled with and driven by a love for God. This verse does not describe a person who merely obeys some of the obvious outward commandments found in the Bible. Rather, it defines the parameters of a heart whose great joy in life is found in God alone. As one old-time writer said about the great commandment: "Only think what immense changes would take place on earth, by the world-wide keeping of only (this) one commandment of our God.... (It) has enough in it to turn this almost demonized world into a veritable paradise."[7]

Love is also used to describe other passions as well. Jesus said, "And this is the judgment, that the light is come into the world, and men loved the darkness rather than the light; for their deeds were evil." (John 3:19) He also said, "He who loves his life loses it; and he who hates his life in this world shall keep it to life eternal." (John 12:25) Paul spoke of those who were lovers of money (1 Timothy 6:10), lovers of self (2 Timothy 3:1), and "lovers of pleasure rather than lovers of God." (2 Timothy 3:4) He also mentioned the abandonment of his close comrade Demas, "having loved this present world, has deserted me and gone to Thessalonica." (2 Timothy 4:10)

When John said, "If anyone loves the world, the love of the Father is not in him," he was describing the narrow path and the broad way. Will the primary recipient of his devotion be God? Or will he selfishly devote himself to pursuing the flesh-gratifying things this world has to offer him? The devil attempts to paint gray what God paints black and white. Some may say that the believer should not love the things of this world *too* much, but John said that we are not to love the things of this world *at all*! If someone is into what this world system offers, he simply does not love God. The Bible is quite clear concerning this.*

Jesus put it in the most unequivocal terms when He said, "No one can serve two masters; for either he will hate the one and love the other, or he will hold to one and despise the other. You cannot serve God and mammon." (Matthew 6:24) In spite of the fact that the enemy has used sooth-saying preachers to gloss over these clear-cut statements, it cannot be any plainer: a person will either serve his lust for what the world offers, or he will serve a holy desire to please his God.

THE GREAT DECEPTION

The devil's ceaseless aim is the deception of Christ's followers, causing them to believe they can live for the world's rewards and still maintain a viable walk with God at the same time. To a large extent, this deception is already firmly entrenched in the Church and is paving the way for an even greater deception to follow. It has been so subtle in its approach and so universal in its extent that this insidious plot remains practically invisible as it rapidly unfolds. To come to grips with the magnitude of what is happening in the spirit realm, it will require an open heart and a relentless determination to obtain truth.

Satan's multifaceted ploys continually work together with the carnal desires of man to achieve his desired goal. His capability to mask the truth and blind the mind should never be underestimated! (2 Corinthians 4:4) "Satan disguises himself as an angel of light." (2 Corinthians 11:14) As already mentioned, people are deceived when their desire for the world exceeds their desire for truth. Dear one, in the most unambiguous language, the apostle Paul warned believers that the spirit of

---

* I don't mean to imply that a true believer cannot or does not enjoy hobbies or interests outside of the Lord. What is being discussed here are passions that rule a person's heart and life.

Antichrist is coming "with all the deception of wickedness for those who perish, because they did not receive the love of the truth so as to be saved." (2 Thessalonians 2:10) You must have a love of the truth no matter what it may cost you!

Kosmos is God's enemy. It has turned its back upon the Lord and openly defied His authority. It is a wolf in sheep's clothing, stalking through our churches, bookstores and homes, constantly, untiringly, and persistently attempting to deceive, tempt, influence and oppose God's people. It presents itself as our friend, but it is an extremely evil being bent on our destruction. His efforts will increase and intensify as Christ's return draws nearer. (Revelation 12:12)

American Christians cannot afford to forget it was the spirit of the world that murdered Jesus, and Paul, and eleven of the disciples, and it will murder anyone else who attempts to stand against it. (John 15:18-20) Embedded in the lust-laden American lifestyle of the 21st century is an unseen enemy constantly appealing to their lower natures, persistently trying to seduce and deceive them, and viciously attacking anyone who doesn't conform. In earlier centuries thousands of saints chose to die horrible deaths rather than compromise or renounce their faith in Jesus Christ. One might wonder where this sobriety is in today's Church. Where are the true witnesses for Christ?

The following catalog of biblical statements about the world should serve to sober and awaken us. Throughout this book, we will methodically examine most of these passages in their entirety in an attempt to apply them in a practical way to modern Christianity. For now, they are listed in their barest form, allowing for the full impact of what is being expressed.

+ My kingdom is not of this world. (John 18:36)
+ The world has been crucified to me. (Galatians 6:14)
+ You formerly walked according to the course of this

world. (Ephesians 2:2)

+ Do not be bound together with unbelievers.
  (2 Corinthians 6:14)
+ Keep yourself unstained by the world. (James 1:27)
+ Do not be conformed to this world. (Romans 12:2)
+ Come out from their midst and be separate.
  (2 Corinthians 6:17)
+ Do not love the world, nor the things in the world.
  (1 John 2:15)
+ If anyone loves the world, the love of the Father is not in
  him. (I John 2:15)
+ Demas, having loved this present world, has deserted me.
  (2 Timothy 4:10)
+ A friend of the world makes himself an enemy of God.
  (James 4:4)
+ Gain the whole world, and forfeit your soul. (Mark 8:36)
+ He who loves his life [in this world] loses it. (John 12:25)
+ Our struggle is against the world forces of this darkness.
  (Ephesians 6:12)
+ Whatever is born of God overcomes the world. (1 John 5:4)
+ They have escaped the defilements of the world.
  (2 Peter 2:20)
+ The world has hated them. (John 17:14)
+ They are not of the world. (John 17:14)
+ Men of whom the world was not worthy. (Hebrews 11:38)
+ Do not marvel, brethren, if the world hates you.
  (1 John 3:13)

But before we tackle the practical ways in which all of us are being affected, let's investigate the conspiracy itself. We must go deeper to unmask what strategy the spirit of the world will use in the dark days which lie ahead. We must trace its workings all the way back to its origin (to the early days of man).

"O universal strength, I know it well,
It is but froth of folly to rebel;
For thou art Lord and hast the keys of Hell."[1]
-C.S. Lewis

2

The Origin of Babylon

The climax to the Book of Revelation and the history of mankind is the ultimate battle between the forces of good and evil known as Armageddon. In this great clash of forces, the followers of Antichrist will gather for a showdown with God, pitting Satan's psychotic illusions of grandeur against the Kingdom of the lowly Jesus. It will be the devil's final attempt at overthrowing the authority of God in this world.

As a symbol of the forces of evil, John was shown a city called Babylon. Though many have argued that Babylon refers to an actual modern-day city, such as Rome, New York, or even the ancient city of Babylon rebuilt, it actually represents the entire fallen world. Babylon symbolizes the gathering together of all those who want to rid themselves of God's presence and authority.

One might wonder why our Lord chose Babylon to represent the ungodly world of the last days. Why not Rome, who controlled the world with an iron grip, murdering and torturing those who chose to follow Christ? Why not the city of Corinth, a cesspool of immorality? Or why not Egypt, the country that once held the Hebrew people in bondage for four hundred years? Or Sodom and Gomorrah, the twin cities of homosexuality and perversion? Why did He choose to portray the fallen world in the last days as Babylon?

For us to comprehend properly the significance of what the Lord is unveiling about what will transpire in the end times, we must first examine the origin and spirit of ancient Babylon as it relates to all of biblical history.

THE FOUNDING OF THE WORLD'S FIRST POST-FLOOD CITY

Babylon's origins are described in Genesis Ten, following the account of the Great Flood. Noah's sons were told to "be fruitful and multiply, and fill the earth." (Genesis 9:1) God separated them so that they would scatter around the world. His sons were blessed with children, and their children had more children.

Among the descendants of Ham came a great-grandson of Noah named Nimrod, who "became a mighty one on the earth. He was a mighty hunter *before* the Lord.... And the beginning of his kingdom was Babel." (Genesis 10:9-10) The Hebrew word for "before," *paniym*, has a variety of applications, but its root (*paneh*), signifies "to face." The context of its usage here seems to connote the idea of doing something in outright defiance of another: "in a person's face," we would say. This would make perfect sense if what some scholars say is true: the "name Nimrod comes from *marad*, 'he rebelled.'"[2] Nimrod's actions were a deliberate snubbing of God's authority, comparable to a junior officer committing mutiny against a ship's captain.

The story of Nimrod, and subsequently of Babel (later known as Babylon), is a tale that must be explored if we are to grasp the significance of Babylon the Great in the last days. Apparently Nimrod was an extremely violent man, bent on dominating and ruling over the lives of others in direct defiance of the Lord's wishes. It must be understood that God's presence and authority were established on the earth through the lives of Shem and his descendants. His was a godly line, a people who were to some degree subjected to the rule of the Lord in their lives. Nimrod wanted no part of this and set out to establish something hitherto unknown: a kingdom of his own with himself as its ruler.

To learn the whole story of this insurgent, we must turn to early historians who had access to ancient writings long since lost to man. The Targum, a loose translation of the O.T. into Aramaic before the time of Christ, translated First Chronicles 1:10 as follows: "Nimrod began to be a mighty man in sin, a murderer of innocent men, and a rebel before the Lord."[3] This same perspective of Nimrod* is given by Trogus Pompeius when he said that he, "first of all changed the contended moderation of the ancient manners, incited by a new passion, the desire of conquest. He was the first who carried on war against his neighbors, and he conquered all nations from Assyria to Lybia, as they were yet unacquainted with the arts of war."[4] Justin, an early Christian martyr, said the following about Nimrod: "Having subdued, therefore, his neighbors, when, by an accession of forces, being still further strengthened, he went forth against other tribes, and every new victory paved the way for another, he subdued all the peoples of the East."[5]

Until this time, men had been content to live as nomadic tent-dwellers, which was exactly what God desired. He well knew what lay dormant in the hearts of humans and the intensification of evil sure to occur if men began to congregate in cities. Nimrod chose to build the world's first city in a fertile valley of Mesopotamia.

---

* This and some of the other ancient quotes were stated of one Ninus, recognized by scholars as another name of Nimrod.

Nimrod's rebellion against God's order aroused the admiration of others who shared his enmity. He was quick to seize this advantage and use it for his own selfish ambitions. "Come, let us build for ourselves a city," he said to his followers, "and a tower whose top will reach into heaven, and let us make for ourselves a name; lest we be scattered abroad over the face of the whole earth." (Genesis 11:4)

This tower, the first of a long line of man-made spectacles on earth, was designed to attract other people of like mind. Nimrod clearly wanted to entice people to himself and away from God. He offered them an alternative to the dull life of serving the Lord in the quiet fields of the wilderness.[†] The tower of Babel was intended to be a wonder in the world. Nimrod's aim was to erect a monument symbolic of man's abilities without God. The result was an ancient skyscraper that became the emblem of their greatness and collective achievement. Josephus, the Jewish historian of the first century, records what he knew of the story.

Now it was Nimrod who excited them to such an affront and contempt of God. He was the grandson of Ham, the son of Noah, a bold man, and of great strength of hand. He persuaded them not to ascribe it to God, as if it was through his means they were happy, but to believe that it was their own courage which procured that happiness. He also gradually changed the government into tyranny, seeing no other way of turning men from the fear of God, but to bring them into a constant dependence on his power. He also said he would be revenged on God, if he should have a mind to drown the world again; for that he would build a tower too high for the waters to be able to reach! and that he would avenge himself on God for destroying their forefathers!

---

† The wilderness was the place where Moses, David and many others would later come into a tremendous knowledge of God.

Now the multitude were very ready to follow the determination of Nimrod, and to esteem it a piece of cowardice to submit to God; and they built a tower, neither sparing any pains, nor being in any degree negligent about the work: and, by reason of the multitude of hands employed in it, it grew very high, sooner than any one could expect; but the thickness of it was so great, and it was so strongly built, that thereby its great height seemed, upon the view, to be less than it really was. It was built of burnt brick, cemented together with mortar[‡] made of bitumen, that it might not be liable to admit water.[6]

The city of Babel quickly established itself as a place where men could unite in pursuit of their own lusts and desires. With the help of each other, in an unholy alliance, they would achieve what none of them could alone. Upon establishing Babel, Nimrod went on to found three other cities in the immediate area known as Shinar (c.f. Genesis 10:10). Thus, he not only founded the world's first city,[§] but he also began its first confederation of cities; i.e. an actual nation.[⊄]

Nimrod's followers must have been in awe of his leadership and organizational abilities, idolizing him as a "national" hero. Of course, he was more than willing to accept their adoration. He, rather than God, would now be the focal point of their worship.

A NEW RELIGION

Apparently, Nimrod perceived that in order to succeed in his insurrection, he would need a powerful force to unite

---

‡ Harrison brings out that this was the first time brick and mortar are used, in contrast with the more primitive use of stones.

§ Babylon was at least the world's first post-Flood city.

⊄ After the Lord's intervention at Babel, Nimrod ventured west into the area later known as Assyria and founded more cities, not the least of which was Nineveh. (c.f. Genesis 10:11-12)

his diverse subjects. Perhaps this was an additional motive for building the Tower of Babel. Not only would it rise higher than any future flood, but it would also serve as a focal point for a new religion! The tower would serve both as a magnificent attraction to draw people from all over the world as well as a temple to gods of their own choosing. His people would no longer be confined to worship *only* the Great Jehovah who caused the Flood. Nimrod's new temple would allow people to worship a host of "gods."

It is probable this was the result of a brilliant revelation: Jehovah was only one of many gods! "Of course," Nimrod might have told his followers, "Jehovah is the god of the Semites (the descendants of Shem), but surely there are many other deities that affect the lives of mankind." It seems that the founder of Babylon presented a vast array of gods to whom his subjects could appeal for help.

It is important to note that this idea was not really Nimrod's brainchild. His revelation had to originate from an intelligence far greater than his own. Henry Morris, who does an excellent job of tracing modern humanism and evolution back to this period of rebellion, discusses the origin of idolatry:

> The remarkable complex of astrology, spiritism, mythology, polytheistic idolatry, and evolutionary pantheism has been variously masked in pseudo-scientific verbiage and humanistic speculation (something for every taste!), which marked the ancient religions as well as modern evolutionary scientism. This worldview could never have been devised by men alone, not even such powerful men as Nimrod and his followers. The supernatural hold that this system has maintained over multitudes through the ages surely implies nothing less than a supernatural origin.

Somehow, in connection with the building of that first pagan temple at the peak of Babel's Tower, Satan and his powers of darkness must have communicated these occultic revelations to Nimrod, setting the first great post-Flood rebellion against God under way. That rebellion was interrupted for a time by the Babel judgment, but it continues today world-wide, stronger than ever in history.[7]

No doubt Nimrod's early religion was an uncomplicated one. Both biblical reference and archaeological evidence reveal that early man worshiped "the host of heaven." This expression, found frequently in the O.T., literally means "army of the sky." "In the astrological cults of antiquity it was believed that celestial bodies were animated by spirits and thus constituted a living army that controlled heavenly destiny."[8] It is probable that the earliest forms of idolatry involved the planets. From the lofty heights of the ziggurat of Babel, Sumerian priests could study the movement of the planets. At first, this primarily consisted of the sun, moon and five planets, which were all worshiped as gods. From these simple beginnings sprang the pseudo-science of astrology.

The basic premise of astrology was (and is) that the movements of the planets affect the lives of earth-dwellers. Astrologers eventually became so adept at studying the "zodiac," they believed they could actually foretell future events in individuals' lives by comparing the position of the heavenly bodies within the zodiac at the time of their births. This "science," of course, has developed over the course of many generations, but apparently it was first conceived in the mystery religions of ancient Babylon.

Nimrod's domain continued to grow, as did his power. His position as king of Babylon (which by now had become a country) enabled him to collect a harem for himself, out of which emerged a young concubine who distinguished herself above the rest. She was a lusty beauty named Semiramis whom Nimrod made queen of his kingdom. Immediately following Nimrod's death, Semiramis consolidated power and took control over the empire. Her first official act as queen of Babylon was to deify her deceased husband. His followers had idolized him in life, and she exalted him in death.

It seems that the licentious behavior of Semiramis was no secret in the court of Babylon. Eventually, she conceived a child and concocted a brilliant scheme to mask her promiscuous deeds. She announced that Nimrod had risen from the dead and was the child's father! Her son, Tammuz, was then glorified as a god-man on earth. Many believe that the story of Nimrod, Semiramis, and Tammuz became the prototype for many (if not all) of the ancient mythologies and fertility cults that would blossom over the next several thousand years. What began and developed in Babylon and Nineveh, eventually spread (through the great dispersion God caused by confusing their languages) to Canaan, Egypt and eventually to Greece and Rome. In every ancient civilization the identical mythologies abound—each with their own particular nuances—but essentially the same. The fertility cults, which evolved from this initial myth, had even greater consequences upon mankind than that of astrology.

Of these ancient myths, the one which revolved around the violent death of Tammuz is especially significant. Whether he is named Osiris in Egyptian folklore, Bacchus in Greek and Roman, or Balder in Norse, it is the same basic tale. Tammuz is killed and finds himself in the abode of the dead. Horrified over his demise, the other gods offer a ransom to the goddess of Hell for his release. She agrees, but on one condition: everything on earth must weep for him. Only then could it be proven that he is truly worthy to return to earth.

Accordingly, one of the rites of the primitive cults was the weeping for Tammuz. We even find this practice mentioned in Scripture when Ezekiel is transported in the Spirit (from Babylon of all places!) to Jerusalem, where he is shown women weeping for Tammuz. (Ezekiel 8:14) Semiramis and Tammuz seem to have impacted Christian dogma, as the myths surrounding their lives would pave the way for much of the Roman Catholic concept of Madonna: Mary the Mother of God.[9]

Ancient Fertility Cults

As has already been noted, Semiramis was a very lewd and wicked woman. Apparently, it was her depraved imagination that conceived the idea of introducing gross sexual immorality into the religious rites practiced in Babylonian idolatry. Many of these original idolatries would later be labeled as "fertility cults."

Babylonian girls were raised to believe the religious teachings of these cults. In this Babylonian culture, young virgins were expected to make themselves available to be used by the Sumerian priests to initiate worship of their gods and to collect "offerings." Rex Andrews provides us a fuller understanding of this wretched practice:

> They also offered the most precious gifts they could devote: their virginity, chastity, and sense of modesty and shame.... The pathways and steps of the temple were infested with women of all ages, offering themselves to passers by.
>
> The Babylonians were not the only people to be sunk in this degrading sin. The whole world, all peoples, races, and lands, polluted themselves with it. From the Caspian Sea to the isles of Greece; from the mountains of Ararat to the deserts of Yemen and beyond. Every knee bowed to the goddess, every hand was stretched out to her imploringly; her name on every lip.
>
> One of the hallowed fundamentals of the worship of Ishtar obliged every woman who believed in her and worshipped in her Temple, to give herself at least once in her life to a strange man. This obligation was universal

without respect to age or rank. Every female worshipper had to sit in the sanctuary with veiled face and expose her nakedness to the lustful eyes of strange males. If a man halted in front of a woman and desired to have intercourse with her, he would, as a sign of his desire, place a piece of silver or some article of value in her bosom. The woman was then compelled to surrender to his lust. This gift was taken by the priests as an offering to the goddess Ishtar.

Besides this compulsory whoredom which was carried on by the priests of Ishtar, there were attached to the Temple permanent harlot votaries, or kedeshot (viz: holy, sanctified to Ishtar for harlotry.) During the spring festival, when Ishtar descended into Sheol (made into a theatrical) to beg the shades to release Tammuz from the bonds of deathly slumber and send him back to earth to renew its fruitfulness and fertility, the kedeshot participated in the wildest orgies in the Temple in honor of the returning newborn Tammuz.[10]

As time went on, the licentious nature of Semiramis came to be personified in different cultures by the names Astarte, Ishtar, Aphrodite, and Venus. Subsequently, as mythology developed in different civilizations, imaginative followers contrived a variety of stories about the various gods and goddesses.

Perhaps we can now better understand why this ancient city was called "MYSTERY, BABYLON THE GREAT, THE MOTHER OF HARLOTS AND ABOMINATIONS OF THE EARTH." (Revelation 17:5 KJV—capitals in the original biblical manuscripts.) We are all aware that the term "harlot" is used in the Bible to illustrate idolatry. As we can see above, and from Israel's history of involvement with fertility cults, the harlotries of Babylon also contain an element of literal truth as well. With the exception of Islam, the religion that Nimrod began spawned every false religion the world has known. Thus, Babylon is called the "mother" of harlots and abominations.

But more importantly, Babylon resurrected the rebellion, which had filled the hearts of men prior to the Flood. What began in the heart of an audacious rebel grew into a cancer, destined to spread across the earth.

"Depart from me, evildoers, that I may observe the commandments of my God."
-The Psalmist (119:115)

3

WORLDLINESS: THE DOWNFALL OF ISRAEL

About a decade after the death of Nimrod (and less than 300 years after the Great Flood), Abraham was born in Ur, one of the cities Nimrod built in Mesopotamia. We may assume that the knowledge of God was still very prevalent upon earth. There were probably no atheists in those days, only rebels who were flocking to the newly created fertility cults of Babel. Although godly men like Job (who also lived in this general time period) continued to seek the Lord, most of the inhabitants of Mesopotamia descended into the depths of immorality, carnality, and rebellion against God's authority.

As difficult as it may have been for the Lord to reach anyone in Ur with the truth, God broke through to Abraham and revealed Himself powerfully to him. The Scriptures are silent about his early years, but we do know that when he was about seventy years old the Lord appeared to him, saying, "Depart from your country and your relatives, and *come into* the land that I will show you." (Acts 7:2-3) "By faith Abraham, when he was called, obeyed by *going out* to a place which he was to receive for an inheritance; and he *went out*, not knowing where he was going." (Hebrews 11:8)

And so it was that Abraham was *called out* of "the world" of Ur, which the evil, seditious Nimrod had established a few decades before. For the next 105 years the transient patriarch lived in tents and refused to settle for the more comfortable lifestyle of the godless culture around him. His life would prove to be an example of godliness for centuries to come.

Abraham's nephew Lot also expressed faith in God and joined him on his trek into unfamiliar territory. Together, the two families left Mesopotamia, going first to Syria and then on to Canaan. However, Lot's faith did not measure up to his uncle's. As the two householders expanded their flocks and herds in Canaan, Lot's servants strove with Abraham's servants to the point that the tension was no longer tolerable. Finally Abraham said to Lot, "Please let there be no strife between you and me, nor between my herdsmen and your herdsmen, for we are brothers. Is not the whole land before you? Please *separate* from me: if to the left, then I will go to the right; or if to the right, then I will go to the left." (Genesis 13:8-9)

This was a wake-up call to Lot and his wife. They should have humbled themselves to their godly uncle and repented. Their attitude should have been like that of Ruth when Naomi told her to return to her own people: "Do not urge me to leave you or turn back from following you; for where you go, I will go, and where you lodge, I will lodge. Your people shall be my people, and your God, my God. Where you die, I will die, and there I will be buried. Thus may the LORD do to me, and worse, if anything but death parts you and me." (Ruth 1:16-17) Instead of seeing the life in God they could have through the guidance of Abraham, their focus was elsewhere:

And Lot lifted up his eyes and saw all the valley of the Jordan, that it was well watered everywhere—this was before the LORD destroyed Sodom and Gomorrah—like the garden of the LORD, like the land of Egypt as you go to Zoar. So Lot chose for himself all the valley of the Jordan; and Lot journeyed eastward. Thus they separated from each other. Abram settled in the land of Canaan, while Lot settled in the cities of the valley, and moved his tents as far as Sodom. Now the men of Sodom were wicked exceedingly and sinners against the LORD. (Genesis 13:10-13)

Had the love of city life in Ur been purged from Lot's heart? Apparently not, for he was drawn toward Sodom. Not only was it more convenient to live amongst other people, but the land was also more lush. The fact that Sodom and Gomorrah were extremely vile was of secondary importance to Lot; like many who claim to be followers of Christ today, the benefits of such a union were too good to pass up—*his religion would have to fit around his love of this world.* Lot moved his family near Sodom, while Abraham settled in the more western part of Canaan where life was rural and carnal pleasures sparse.

Not long after Abraham and Lot parted ways, five rival kings plundered Sodom and Gomorrah, carrying Lot and his family into slavery. Abraham immediately set out in pursuit of the warlords, following them to Dan, where he and his men routed them. This was the only military action Abraham ever took—not for his own sake but to save his wayward nephew and family.

This was the second wake-up call the Lord graciously sent to Lot and his wife. Living outside the will of God is dangerous! This carnal couple should have humbled themselves, acknowledged their folly, and showed their repentance by leaving Sodom once and for all. There was certainly plenty of room in Canaan for both families to live comfortably. Would not God have met Lot's need and blessed him as He did Abraham? But Lot did not learn a needed lesson from this near tragedy. Rather, he now moved his family *into* Sodom, where they remained for another ten years, until the day the angels of the Lord came to judge that wicked place.

Once again, it was Abraham who saved his fleshly relatives from destruction by "standing before the Lord" to intercede for them. Even though Lot was a "believer," his actions during this experience reveal that he had drifted far from the Lord in his heart. He did offer to shelter the angels from the homosexual gang who stormed his house, but turned around and offered the sex-crazed mob his virgin daughters to appease their lust! Mercifully the angels stepped in and blinded the men at the door, averting yet another tragedy caused by Lot's poor judgment. Lot's warning the next day to his sons-in-law brought only scorn, as it always does when the warning messenger is worldly and his life with God is lukewarm, compromising, and lacking in authority.

When the angelic messengers urgently pressed Lot to leave at once, "he hesitated." The Hebrew word for hesitate means "reluctant to move." Lot's wife did not want to leave her beloved Sodom at all, and it seems Lot was leaving only with the utmost reluctance. Had it not been for the compassion of the Lord who directed the angels to seize their hands and drag them out of the city, they all would have been destroyed! Once outside the city, the angels told them, "Escape for your life! Do not look behind you, and do not stay anywhere in the valley; escape to the mountains, lest you be swept away." (Genesis 19:17) Rather than rushing his family into safety, Lot sought for a compromise. "I cannot escape to the mountains, lest the disaster overtake me and I die; now behold, this town is near enough to flee to, and it is small. Please, let me escape there (is it not small?) that my life may be saved." (Genesis 19:19-20) The nearby town of Zoar was probably just as wicked as Sodom and Gomorrah. Nevertheless, the angel acquiesced, saying, "Behold, I grant you this request also, not to overthrow the town of which you have spoken. Hurry, escape there, for I cannot do anything until you arrive there." (Genesis 19:21-22)

The molten sulfur, which fell like a rain of fire on the wicked and godless cities of the Jordan Valley, destroyed them completely and buried them under a layer of salt. Lot's wife, even more backslidden than he was, lingered and looked back longingly, and the falling sulfur turned her body into a perpetual memorial to the love of this world. Nearly 2,000 years later Jesus used her tragic story to warn our generation: "On that day, let not the one who is on the housetop and whose goods are in the house go down to take them away; and likewise let not the one who is in the field turn back. Remember Lot's wife." (Luke 17:31-32) She was an example of what *not* to do in life. Instead of being saved from destruction, her love for this world brought about her demise. As is always the case, her heart had remained with her treasure.

Lot lived on with his two daughters—which was all he had left after his years of greed in Sodom—choosing to live in a mountain cave above the town of Zoar instead of humbling himself to live with Abraham. His daughters, spiritually polluted by a lifetime of exposure to Sodom's wicked environment, devised a plan so typical of fleshly thinking. With no prospects of marriage left to them, they arranged to conceive children by their own father, who unknowingly impregnated them while in a drunken state at their instigation. Two sons named Moab and Ammon were the result of this sordid affair. It goes without saying that the Moabites and Ammonites would cause the people of God tremendous grief for hundreds of years to come.*

Lessons from Sodom

Can you see how the characters in this story typify the different kinds of people who are in our churches today?

---

* This story shows the devastating effects one man's folly can have on the lives of other people.

First, there is Abraham, a man of great faith and consecration. God respected his level of consecration to such a degree that, before He would destroy the cities of the Jordan Valley, He felt compelled to inform Abraham. "Shall I hide from Abraham," He asked the angels, "what I am about to do?" (Genesis 18:17) Then, as the Lord sent the angels to execute judgment, Abraham, full of God's mercy, began to intercede for the wicked inhabitants of these two infamous cities. He pleaded, He bargained, He cried out on their behalf. So powerful was his intercession with God that we are later told, Lot was saved *only* because of Abraham. (Genesis 19:29) His prayers had such an impact in heaven that the angel told Lot, "Hurry, escape there, for I cannot do anything until you arrive there." (Genesis 19:22)

Second, there is Lot. His love of worldly prosperity led him away from the Promised Land and the spiritual covering of Abraham in favor of the entertaining, sensuous city-life. Rather than leading his family in a life of godliness, he led them straight into the hellish environment of Sodom and Gomorrah. His life typifies the modern professing Christian who has a certain belief in God but never surrenders his will, his life, or his love for this world. He represents the pseudo-believer who follows the Lord only on his own terms. Instead of looking to the godly example of Abraham, Lot made the awful mistake of exaggerating his level of godliness by comparing his life to the lives of the unsaved around him.

Believers today face this same temptation. Our country is practically a mirror image of the wickedness in which Sodom and Gomorrah boasted. No wonder it is so easy for lukewarm Christians to see themselves as godly. As long as their level of purity hovers one notch above this wicked world, they can consider themselves as godly. Yes, compared to the vile men of Sodom, Lot was considered righteous because of his faith. It is also true that God rescued him, but he had to be practically pulled out of Sodom in order to be saved. The tragic consequences of Lot's decisions—the death of his wife and sons-in-law and the corruption of his daughters—should serve as a warning to any believers who imagine they too can love this world system without regret.

Our third example is Lot's wife, whom Jesus solemnly warns us to remember. This woman illustrates the person who sits in an evangelical church listening to godly teaching and preaching but who has never had a genuine conversion. The words of J.C. Ryle apply so accurately to such people:

I will speak of the religious privileges which Lot's wife enjoyed....

Not one in a hundred perhaps had such good example, such spiritual society, such clear knowledge, such plain warnings of Lot's wife. Compared with millions of her fellow-creatures in her time, Lot's wife was a favored woman....

Yet what good effect had all these privileges on the heart of Lot's wife? None at all. Notwithstanding all her opportunities and means of grace—notwithstanding all her special warnings and messages from heaven—she lived and died graceless, godless, and impenitent, and unbelieving. The eyes of her understanding were never opened; her conscience was never really aroused and quickened; her will was never really brought into a state of obedience to God; her affections were never really set on things above. The form of religion which she had was kept up for fashion's sake and not from feeling: it was a cloak worn for the sake of pleasing her company, but not from any sense of its value. She did as others around her in Lot's house: she conformed to her husband's ways; she made no opposition to his religion; she allowed herself to be passively towed along in his wake; but all this time her heart was wrong in the sight of God. The world was in her heart, and her heart was in the world. In this state she lived, and in this state she died.... Nothing so hardens the heart of man as a barren familiarity with sacred things."[1]

Of all the Old Testament examples that Jesus could have selected, it is the example of Lot's wife which He used as a sober warning to those of us living in the last days. God "will not always strive with us" (Psalm 103:9) but will bring swift judgment to those who refuse the way of escape He offers. He commands us to "Remember Lot's wife." How shall we do that? By bringing her story frequently to our remembrance and considering her life in relation to our own. The lesson to be learned from this woman can be summed up in the words Jesus spoke on another occasion: "For where your treasure is, there will your heart be also.... You cannot serve God and mammon." (Matthew 6:21, 24)

A New People

By the time Abraham's grandson, Jacob, and his sons joined Joseph in Egypt, it was teeming with the idolatry which had begun in Mesopotamia long before. The primordial family of Israel walked right into a spiritual cesspool of darkness and remained there for over four hundred years. However, it was not Egyptian wickedness that compelled the Hebrews to seek to escape the land of the Nile. In fact, there is no record of a solitary complaint from them concerning the fertility cults that permeated their newfound society. Rather, they only desired freedom from slavery; it seems these early Israelites cried out to the "god" of their forefathers only because they had nowhere or no one else in which to turn. They themselves were steeped in the same polytheistic idolatry previously discussed that was rampant all over the world: the belief that there were many gods, each of which possessed some unique power or characteristic. The monumental problem they faced was that they were outsiders and could not turn to Egyptian gods for help. Their only hope was to turn to Jehovah, the God of their forefathers—Abraham, Isaac, and Jacob.

The Lord had a plan, of course, and placed a Hebrew boy in Pharaoh's palace who would be trained in all the wisdom of the Egyptians. God's ways are not the ways of man. We are told that, "By faith Moses, when he had grown up, refused to be called the son of Pharaoh's daughter; choosing rather to endure ill-treatment with the people of God, than to enjoy the passing pleasures of sin; considering the reproach of Christ greater riches than the treasures of Egypt; for he was looking to the reward. By faith he left Egypt, not fearing the wrath of the king; for he endured, as seeing Him who is unseen." (Hebrews 11:24-27) God delivered His people, not by human ingenuity and political connections, but by *faith*. The man selected by the Lord to lead them in this great emancipation did not seek a higher position in Pharaoh's court but chose instead to walk away from it all and identify himself with the downtrodden Hebrews—chose to *come out* from among the oppressors and enter into the yoke of the oppressed.

It took forty years in the wilderness for God to purge Moses of the Egyptian mentality and to build into him the meekness that is characteristic of a conquered will. Finally, having molded His vessel into an instrument He could use, the Lord sent him back to Egypt for the deliverance of his brethren. The *spirit of Babylon*, however, by now firmly entrenched in the palaces of Egypt, was not about to let God's people go without a violent battle. The prideful and greedy Pharaoh, full of the devil, dug in his heels and refused to acquiesce to the will of Israel's deliverer.

The Great Jehovah pummeled the Egyptians with plague after plague until Pharaoh relented. In a dazzling display of the Almighty's supreme power on earth, the anti-God spirit in control of Egypt was crushed. In the end, the "god" of the Hebrew slaves had shattered the mightiest nation on earth.

Once they had reached the safety of the eastern side of the Red Sea, Israel sang a mighty song of deliverance, led by the prophetess Miriam, Moses' sister. For a short time, the Hebrews rejoiced in this glorious Being who graciously claimed Jacob's seed as His prized possession. Unfortunately, it was only a matter of days before they turned on the Lord, accusing Him of bringing them out into the desert to kill them.

It is really no great surprise that they responded in this way. For hundreds of years they had utterly given themselves over to the fertility cults of Egypt. They were accustomed to serving demons which lured them with sexual orgies and promises of secret powers, only to abuse them in the end with vicious demands, including child sacrifice. They had grown up with the Babylonian mindset of polytheism. Now they were in the wilderness of Sinai with little food and water and no promise of fleshly indulgence. Indeed, this "God," known by only a small handful of them, was offering nothing that appealed to their lower natures.

Rather than seeing a loving God who had just single-handedly delivered them from backbreaking, brutal labor camps, all they could see was an untrustworthy Being who was unwilling to give them the desires of their flesh. They repeatedly rose up in rebellion against Him. Moses tried to reason with them. He told them of the love of God and reiterated His tender mercies. Nevertheless, these people were not interested in a love relationship with Jehovah. They wanted to return to "the flesh-pots of Egypt" even if it meant going back into slavery!

It seemed that the Hebrews went from one crisis to another. Through Moses, God gave them the law, hoping to work into their corrupted souls the godly mindset, values and perspectives of His Kingdom. Over and over the Lord warned His people to repent of their idolatrous practices, to obey the law given at Sinai and to love Him with all their hearts. Nevertheless, when they reached the borders of Canaan, their faith wavered and they simply refused to go in. Consequently, God kept them in the wilderness for forty years—not in retaliation for their rebellion—but to raise a new, undefiled generation; one that was free of the Babylonian influences that permeated ancient cultures. Just before that new generation was to go into "the land of milk and honey," Moses warned them not to be involved in any way with the heathen nations which still lived there:

> You shall make no covenant with them and show no favor to them. Furthermore, you shall not intermarry with them; you shall not give your daughters to their sons, nor shall you take their daughters for your sons. For they will turn your sons away from following Me to serve other gods; then the anger of the LORD will be kindled against you, and He will quickly destroy you...
>
> For you are a holy people to the LORD your God; the LORD your God has chosen you to be a people for His own possession out of all the peoples who are on the face of the earth. (Deuteronomy 7:1-6)

Unfortunately, the next thousand-plus years is one long history of rebellion to God's authority and intermingling with the heathen nations surrounding them. There were bright spots of course—such as David, Josiah and Hezekiah—but for the most part, God's chosen people rejected Him in favor of the self-indulgent pleasures Babylon offered them. Harrison brings this out more fully:

> The Children of Israel wanted to follow Jehovah but also adopt some of the customs of their neighbors. They wanted

to intermarry, dabble in their neighbor's religions, and imitate the political systems they saw around them. They saw nothing wrong with this mixture. "They didn't wipe out those godless cultures as ordered by GOD; Instead they intermarried with the heathen, and in time became just like them" (Ps. 106:34-35 MSG).[2]

He then goes on to compare the effects of cancer to the spirit of the world in the Body of Christ:

Cancer cells have different properties than regular cells. They have lost their ability to control their rate of division. They have become immortal and can grow indefinitely. Cancer cells are also able to invade adjacent normal cells and transform them into cancer cells. This last characteristic is a particularly dangerous trait. Potentially, one cancer cell could invade one hundred healthy, normal cells and transform them into abnormal cancer cells.

Jehovah was not just concerned about false values and mindsets growing within a community. He saw the danger of a nation with Kingdom of God DNA becoming cancerous. He was concerned about the transformation of Israel's culture into a predatory, religious, self-serving system. Unfortunately, this is what we have in part of the Western Church today.

Because the Children of Israel refused to listen to the godly prophets, social and moral corruption resulted.... Solomon neglected to follow the Lord with all his heart. He tried to be politically correct by tolerating other religions in their country. Under Solomon's leadership, anyone could freely worship other gods, including his own wives. This mixture in the land was not a sign of Israel's strength but of its weakness.[3]

After recounting the failure of the Hebrews, Paul said, "Now these things happened to them as an example, and they were written for our instruction, upon whom the ends of the ages have come. Therefore let him who thinks he stands take heed lest he fall." (1 Corinthians 10:11-12)

There are three important lessons for believers today that can be extrapolated from the history of the Jewish people. First, God demands that His people, whether O.T. Jews or N.T. Christians, live a life separated from unbelievers. Second, if they fail to do this, it is inevitable that they will be drawn into the same idolatry that dominates the lives of the ungodly. Third, if and when that happens, God will allow His people to come under the oppression of the very people with whom they have mingled. The clear biblical mandate from God's dealings with the Jewish people is that His people must maintain a distinct and separate lifestyle from those who are a part of the kingdom of darkness.

"Division is better than agreement in evil."[1]
-George Hutcheson

"Let us remember, that whilst we are in this world, we sojourn in a strange land, and are at a distance from our home; and, therefore, do not let us be inordinately affected with anything in it."[2]
-Philip Doddridge

4

"COME OUT!"

T hings could not have looked worse in 445 B.C. for God's chosen people. The northern kingdom of Israel had been taken captive nearly 300 years before, assimilated into Assyrian culture and lost to history's view. The southern kingdom had fallen to Nebuchadnezzar in 586 B.C. and the 70 years of captivity followed exactly as predicted by Jeremiah.

Yet, through Daniel's intercession and the labor of "separated" men like Nehemiah, Ezra, and Haggai, a remnant had returned to the land of Israel to rebuild the walls of Jerusalem and restore the Temple and its worship. In spite of their efforts, many of Babylon's Jews did not want to return! They had prospered and were loath to leave their wealth behind. They loved the good life of the richest city on earth. Why give up the comforts of their adopted home for an uncertain future in the harsh, desolate land of their forefathers?

They were still Jewish, in their view of things and felt they could keep up their religion without "consecrating" to go back, but in reality they were addicted to Babylon and its pleasures.

To such people Isaiah cried, "Depart, depart, go out from there, touch nothing unclean; go out of the midst of her, purify yourselves, you who carry the vessels of the LORD." (Isaiah 52:11) In yet another earnest plea, God was calling His people to *a life of separation*, this time to leave Babylon itself. Notice the command of God for His people to *act*, to *do* something. "Detach yourselves! Break away from the king of Babylon, My people! Sever all your ties to him! And once you have made that separation, purify yourselves from the contamination that has come upon you through your association with him."

That is the background in the Old Testament for the same powerful call of God to His people in New Testament times. "COME OUT!"

Let's take a few moments to explore the connection.

The Kingdom of God underwent a great transformation after Calvary. No longer confined to a single nation, His Kingdom became all-inclusive: "Whosoever will, let him come." From "every tribe and tongue and nation" (Revelation 5:9) God began assembling His people and calling them to a separated life. Their sanctification was not to be the same as that of the Old Testament Jews, living in a closed society, separated entirely from the other nations of the world. No, God's New Testament believers would have to live alongside unbelieving neighbors, shop at worldly stores, work in ungodly businesses, and yet remain detached from the "Babylon" around them; separated *from* the world while living *in* the world—separated *unto* God IN THEIR HEARTS.

Having been delivered "from the domain of darkness, and transferred to the kingdom of His beloved Son," (Colossians 1:13) they would live separated from this world's system, set apart as consecrated vessels for God's use. They would be known as saints, (Greek *hagios*, "separated ones, set apart ones, holy ones"), filled with the Holy Spirit (Greek, *Hagios Pneuma*). "Or do you not know that your body is a temple of the Holy Spirit who is in you, whom you have from God, and that you are not your own? For you have been bought with a price: therefore glorify God in your body," Paul said. (1 Corinthians 6:19-20)

The corporate body of these "separated ones" is called the Church (Greek *ekklesia*, from *ek*, which means *out of*, and *kletos*, which means *called*). In Old Testament language, God's called out ones were "the congregation of the Lord"; in the New Testament they are "the church," the "called out ones." Paul's meaning was unmistakable to the Greek-speaking believers of Corinth in his salutation to them:

Paul, *called* (*kletos*) as an apostle of Jesus Christ by the will of God, and Sosthenes our brother, to the *church* (*ekklesia*) of God which is at Corinth, to those who have been *sanctified* (*hagiazo*) in Christ Jesus, *saints* (*hagios*) by *calling* (*kletos*), with all who in every place call upon the name of our Lord Jesus Christ, their Lord and ours. (1 Corinthians 1:1-2)

Listen to the explanation of the meaning of such words from the pen of W. B. Godbey, a fiery preacher of the 19th Century.

Ekklesia, from *ek*, out, and *kaleo*, to call, means Church throughout the Greek New Testament. If you do not remember that definition you will fall into utter bewilderment on the Church idea, led astray by the Churchism of the present day, which is utterly variant from, and antagonistical to the New Testament *ekklesia*, which consisted only of the souls called out of the world, and separated unto God. Hence, all worldly churches are simply Satan's counterfeits....

This is the glorified Church of the First Born, "without spot or wrinkle." The members of this Church are not joined in, but born into it, by the supernatural intervention of the Holy Ghost. This is none of your worldly Churches, as the very word for Church, *ekklesia*, means *the called out of the world*; while *hagiadzoo*, sanctify, means *to take the world out of you*.

Hence, all the members of the New Testament Church have a double reason for being unworldly; the one because they have come out of the world, and left it; and the other, because the world has been taken out of them. Hence, there is a double divorcement between them and the world.[3] (emphasis added)

This gives us a perspective about the true makeup of the New Testament Church. With these definitions in mind, let us examine closely what it means to be a part of this living spiritual Body. In the following passages found in the Book of Acts, the defining phrase "the called out ones" has been substituted for the word "church":

And on that day a great persecution arose against *the called out ones* in Jerusalem; and they were scattered throughout the regions of Judea and Samaria, except the apostles. (Acts 8:1)

But Saul began ravaging *the called out ones*, entering house after house; and dragging off men and women, he would put them in prison. (Acts 8:3)

So *the called out ones* throughout all Judea and Galilee and Samaria enjoyed peace, being built up; and, going on in the fear of the Lord and in the comfort of the Holy Spirit, [they] continued to increase. (Acts 9:31)

So Peter was kept in prison, but prayer for him was being made fervently by *the called out ones* to God. (Acts 12:5)

"Come Out!"

> Be on guard for yourselves and for all the flock, among which the Holy Spirit has made you overseers, to shepherd *the called out ones* of God which He purchased with His own blood. (Acts 20:28)

The Church of Jesus Christ was born in spectacular fashion; conversions were thorough and remarkable. Conditions before and after salvation were dramatically different. Converts understood that they would face persecution and possibly even death. Can you see how the people of God in the early Church lived in a definite state of separation from the unsaved around them? Those dear people would probably weep if they saw how apathetic and unseparated from the world are God's "called out ones" of today! The author of the Book of Hebrews poses a sobering question to all who profess Christianity: "How much severer punishment do you think he will deserve who has trampled under foot the Son of God, and has regarded as unclean the blood of the covenant by which he was sanctified, and has insulted the Spirit of grace?" (Hebrews 10:29)

The Call of God's People

What happens when a person responds to God's call to enter His Kingdom, and yet retains his ties to the devil's kingdom? Jesus, the One who hung on the Cross to purchase a people for Himself, made it very clear that this is not possible. "No one," He said, "after putting his hand to the plow and looking back, is fit for the kingdom of God." (Luke 9:62) "If anyone comes to Me, and does not hate his own father and mother and wife and children and brothers and sisters, yes, and even his own life, he cannot be My disciple." (Luke 14:26) "He who is not with Me is against Me; and he who does not gather with Me scatters." (Matthew 12:30) Half-hearted devotion to Christ is not merely unacceptable; it is impossible. It takes time for a person's consecration level to mature of course, but it is doubtful whether a person who never changes was ever truly converted in the first place.

Paul faced this compromising attitude in the church located in the wicked port city of Corinth; a place full of sexual sin, Greek pride, and pagan practices. The Corinthian believers were "carnal," Paul said. They wanted to retain their old alliances with the world, while at the same time enjoying the benefits of salvation. Paul wrote about their need to break those ties with the world. Calling to mind the great cry from Isaiah with which we opened this chapter, Paul says,

> Do not be bound together with unbelievers; for what partnership have righteousness and lawlessness, or what fellowship has light with darkness? Or what harmony has Christ with Belial, or what has a believer in common with an unbeliever? Or what agreement has the temple of God with idols?
>
> For we are the temple of the living God; just as God said, "I will dwell in them and walk among them; and I will be their God, and they shall be My people."
>
> "Therefore, come out from their midst and be separate," says the Lord. "And do not touch what is unclean; and I will welcome you. And I will be a father to you, and you shall be sons and daughters to Me," says the Lord Almighty.
>
> Therefore, having these promises, beloved, let us cleanse ourselves from all defilement of flesh and spirit, perfecting holiness in the fear of God. (2 Corinthians 6:14-7:1)

This tremendous passage of Scripture contains 3 commandments, 5 comparisons, and 7 conditional promises. Let's take an in-depth look at the three commandments.

Commandment #1: "Get out of unequal yokes!"

Paul is referring here to an obscure law, which forbade the yoking of an ox with a donkey. (Deuteronomy 22:10) The animals aren't compatible and cannot accomplish a synchronized plowing of a field. Yes, the ox and the donkey can graze together, but they can never work side-by-side in a yoke.

Now Paul applies the law's principle to a believer and an unbeliever. A true Christian has undergone an enormous inward change. God has transformed his values, beliefs, and perspectives, and thus his lifestyle; all of which are now diametrically opposed to those of unbelievers around him. There is no possibility of reconciliation between the two.

Paul then asks, "For what partnership have righteousness and lawlessness, or what fellowship has light with darkness?" How can those who are submitted to God integrate with those who are part of a system which is in rebellion against God? How can the kingdom of light—that place of holiness, purity, and truth—co-exist with the unholy, impure, deceptive kingdom of darkness? They are two different kingdoms eternally separated. THERE IS NO GRAY AREA BETWEEN HEAVEN AND HELL.

Paul is targeting worldliness among believers and probing such issues as,

- Should a daughter of light be married to a son of darkness?
- Should a man who is governed by the precepts of heaven be yoked in a business partnership with one who has pledged allegiance to this world's system?
- Should believers fraternize with unbelievers?

The answer to all these questions is a resounding, "NO!" As Paul admonished the Corinthians before, "Do not be deceived: 'Bad company corrupts good morals.'" (1 Corinthians 15:33)

The one who has been truly saved recognizes the effect bad company has on him, and he consistently avoids unhealthy relationships. He lives his life for the kingdom of heaven and is not enthralled with the world's charms or its charmers. He "does not walk in the counsel of the wicked, nor stand in the path of sinners, nor sit in the seat of scoffers," (Psalm 1:1) because he understands his vulnerability to their influences. This is the separated life of a true believer. This is the thrust of the command: *All "unequally yoked" relationships must end.**

COMMAND #2:
"YOUR LIFESTYLE MUST CHANGE!"

The second commandment is contained in Isaiah's words and quoted by Paul in this Corinthian passage. "Therefore, 'Come out from among them and be separate' says the Lord." This implies a definite distinction between the lifestyles of Christians and unbelievers. Those who do not have an eternal perspective live with shortsighted temporal vision. If there is no afterlife, why not make pleasure, possessions and position the primary purposes of life? Not so for the one who has an eternal perspective. He is a pilgrim on his way to a "city which hath foundations, whose Builder and Maker is God." (Hebrews 11:10 KJV) He is separated from this world and belongs to "a chosen race, a royal priesthood, a holy nation, a people for God's own possession." (1 Peter 2:9) His destiny is heaven and he refuses to come under the sway of the philosophies and dictates of this "present evil world."

As we will more fully examine later, too many believers are immersed in the culture of our day. In fact, it could be said that their lives are not much different than those of the unsaved around them. Like the Jews who assimilated themselves into the Babylonian culture, these believers also must heed the call of God to change their lives and separate themselves from the lifestyle of the wicked. This is a distinct commandment from God to the New Testament saint.

---

* Unequally yoked marriage that has already been consummated is an exception to this. (1 Corinthians 7)

Command #3:
"Decontaminate yourselves!"

"Do not touch what is unclean!... Cleanse [yourselves] from all the defilement of flesh and spirit, perfecting holiness in the fear of God." Is not Paul speaking of the contaminating influences of this fallen world?

Imagine, if you will, a healthy person living in a leper colony. Germs are everywhere: on the furniture, on the walls, on the floors. Those germs are the agents of a hideous, debilitating, and detestable disease. One feels the inside pressure, "Don't touch ANYTHING!"

In spiritual terms, the message to every believer is, "Don't have close contact with anything that is a part of the foul existence of Satan's kingdom! Shun all evil, uncleanness, pollution!"

Kosmos is constantly seeking to transfer its repulsive and diabolical mindset onto believers. It does this primarily through the varied forms of mass media and through the educational system. Any believer who lends his ear to the voice of *kosmos* is going to be affected by it. We have to remember that the spirit of the world appeals to the desires of our lower nature. The pull exerted by those lusts should never be underestimated. The enemy knows how to lure believers into his camp by catering to those ungodly passions.

Here's how it works when it comes to the mass media. The unsuspecting person simply wants to watch television when he gets home from work, for instance. *Kosmos* provides him with a wide variety of entertainment. At the same time his mind goes into a satisfied stupor, he is flooded with a barrage of unholy images and messages. Consequently, a worldly mentality is introduced and reinforced.

And here is how it often works in the field of academia. A young person desires to better himself through education. The spirit of the world provides him with a wealth of knowledge while underhandedly slipping in its own ungodly agenda.

To all this Paul cries out, "Let us cleanse ourselves from all defilement of flesh and spirit, perfecting holiness in the fear of God." We as believers should set up barricades to every avenue the devil seeks to access our minds. The Word of God will daily wash away all the contaminating thoughts as we bathe ourselves in it. Let us decry the tendency in ourselves and in others to merely affiliate with Christianity while at the same time retaining close ties with the spirit of the world.

ENEMIES OF GOD

When someone wishes to immigrate to the United States and become a citizen, he must file the proper applications, take needed tests, and go for interviews—all of which are a part of the necessary procedure. The applicant is also expected to renounce his loyalties to his former country and pledge allegiance to his new homeland.

Some come to America, of course, to use her for their own selfish ambitions and purposes. An example of this occurred in 1979 when Iranian revolutionaries took a number of our diplomats hostage. During that time, patriotism rose to a fever pitch in America. Most of the Iranians who had immigrated to the United States prior to this incident also felt badly about what happened in their former country. Their loyalties lay properly with their new country.

Some Iranian immigrants, however, openly expressed their sympathy for the hostage-takers. The response of patriotic Americans was predictable and right. If these immigrants were in America by our government's good graces; if America had opened its heart and land to them; if they were attending our finest colleges on scholarships; if they were employed at a level unimaginable in Iran; then how could they show sympathy for America's enemies? Where was the gratitude for the bounty of freedoms and opportunities they had been afforded?

But is this not a fair analogy for those who have been allowed entrance into the Kingdom of God, only to withhold their loyalty to it and blatantly disregard the grace, which let them in? To them has been given "the keys of the kingdom." (Matthew 16:19) They have been given "everything pertaining to life and godliness." (2 Peter 1:3) God has given His angels charge over them. (Psalm 91:11) If all that were not enough, He has even given them "the desires of their hearts." (Psalm 37:4) And yet, instead of living the rest of their lives in a grateful awareness of all the kindness God has extended to them, they live in collusion with the enemies of the Lord. Such ingratitude! Is their profession of faith in Jesus Christ all a sham? Have they "received Jesus" only for what they can get out of Him?

Steve Harrison shares similar thoughts:

> Today, Christianity is being offered but without a change of kingdoms.... Many believers have become familiar with the Christian culture. They have learned its language, music, and priorities. They may have followed the rules respectfully and supported a church with their tithe. Nevertheless, despite all these efforts, they are still not citizens of the Kingdom of God. Why? Because their lives demonstrate they have not renounced the kingdom of Babylon and turned from its ways.... There is no dual citizenship status in the Kingdom of God.[4]

Kay Arthur adds, "If you don't plan to live the Christian life totally committed to knowing your God and to walking in obedience to Him, then don't begin, for this is what Christianity is all about. It is a change of citizenship, a change of governments, and a change of allegiance. If you have no intention of letting Christ rule your life, then forget Christianity; it's not for you."[5]

The piercing words of James should bring every wayward soul to his senses. "You adulteresses, do you not know that friendship with the world is hostility toward God? Therefore whoever wishes to be a friend of the world makes himself an enemy of God." (James 4:4) Unfortunately, many people simply refuse to accept the plain meaning of such strong statements, even though it is the Word of God. The enemy has veiled the truth expressed to them, and their minds are blinded. (2 Corinthians 4:3-4) The devil's power over those in his spell neutralizes the Word of God. Such "believers" read the verse mentally, but it does not penetrate because years of worldliness and disobedience have hardened their hearts. Their Christian life is a pretense, but they don't see it as such. The very thought that they could be God's enemy is so ridiculous to them that they refuse to consider the possibility. They see no harm in being engrossed with this world. They will not search their hearts, perhaps because deep within they are afraid of what they will discover. Unwilling to be loosed from the grip the world has on their hearts, they simply ignore or explain away the clear meaning of verses like these.

On the other hand, the believer whose heart is tender reads these verses in James and immediately takes inventory of his motives and actions. Am I allowing the world's thinking to affect me? Do I harbor any lusts by which the enemy can appeal to me? "Show me, Lord, where repentance is needed. Oh God! Purge the love of the world from my heart! Set me apart for Thy great service. Jesus, come and take your rightful place inside me." In short, when such a believer sees evidences of worldliness in his life, he begins to repent until all of it is uprooted and eradicated.

The Eternal Abode

Heaven is not a place for the enemies of God, whether they once had some kind of encounter with Him or not. The world's friend is God's enemy. Imagine such a person dying and going to heaven, the place where righteousness and true holiness dwell. God would be his enemy! The mansions would be the homes of his enemy's followers. The streets of gold, the angels and the songs of worship would only arouse contempt. Sitting on the throne is the One who demanded the allegiance he was unwilling to give. Heaven would be the worst possible place to spend eternity for anyone who is in love with the things of this world. Hell is reserved for those who do not want the yoke of God's authority over their lives. In the words of George Whitefield, "A rebel would be so unhappy in heaven, that he would ask God to let him run down to hell for shelter."

It should not be difficult for us to realize the importance Scripture places on the absolute necessity for Christians to separate themselves from the principalities and powers at work on this dark planet. Nevertheless, we seem to have been stricken with blindness, unable to discern the deliberate rebellion that dominates much of American Christianity. Weak conversions and a compromising lifestyle are the result! And Christians remain enslaved to the pleasure palaces of Satan's kingdom!

But this world is not home to the true believer. He is in a war, behind enemy lines. One day, when these wars have ceased, he will be discharged to go home to his much deserved rest. For now he is constantly aware he is in enemy territory. He loves God and wouldn't think of befriending those who hate Him. Betray God by making alliances with His enemies? Unthinkable! God has saved him, kept him, loved him and blessed him. His loyalty runs deep. He loves God because God first loved him. He doesn't hate people, but he detests and disdains what the world loves. His animosity is like David's, when he wrote:

> O that You would slay the wicked, O God; depart from me, therefore, men of bloodshed. For they speak against You

wickedly, and Your enemies take Your name in vain. Do I not hate those who hate You, O LORD? And do I not loathe those who rise up against You? I hate them with the utmost hatred; they have become my enemies. (Psalm 139:19-22)

This must be the conviction of every true believer concerning *kosmos*. This world is *not* home for the follower of Christ. Christians must be like the American diplomats in Iran during the hostage crisis, continuing to hold their American perspectives and values, despite the apparent power of their captors. They still had obligations and duties to uphold; their loyalties remained with their home country.

Paul said, "For our citizenship is in heaven, from which also we eagerly wait for a Savior, the Lord Jesus Christ." (Philippians 3:10) Peter said, "Beloved, I urge you as aliens and strangers to abstain from fleshly lusts, which wage war against the soul." (1 Peter 2:9) The writer of Hebrews said, referring to Abraham, "By faith he lived as an alien in the land of promise, as in a foreign land, dwelling in tents with Isaac and Jacob, fellow heirs of the same promise; for he was looking for a city which has foundations, whose architect and builder is God." (Hebrews 11:9-10)

To be a part of the true, living Church of Jesus Christ does not mean one has joined the ranks of the evangelical movement. It does not mean he has had some kind of spiritual experience in the past and now lives on the fringes of Christianity. Nor does it mean he has incorporated the ideology of the American evangelical movement into his life. It means he is a saint, devoted to and set apart for the Master's use. He has been *called out* of *kosmos* and divorced himself from her. While he has not yet achieved sinless perfection, the longing of his heart is to be conformed to the holy image of Jesus Christ.

"We have learned to live with unholiness
and have come to look upon it as the
natural and expected thing."[1]
-A. W. Tozer

"Our calling, before and above
everything else, is to holiness."[2]
-Andrew Murray

"There is no detour to holiness. Jesus Christ came to
the resurrection through the cross, not around it."[3]
-Leighton Ford

5

BE HOLY AS I AM HOLY

There was a time, not too long ago, when Christians knew from example the meaning of true holiness. Most believers in the early part of the 1900s were very careful to examine all their actions in the light of God's Word. They possessed a reverence and fear of God that caused them to take great care over the way they lived their lives. They realized and embraced the fact that this righteous God was, indeed, HOLY. Within their hearts was a sincere longing for His holiness. They were willing to be "a peculiar people."

For some, this meant absolutely no drinking or dancing. Others even refused to wear make-up or jewelry. Followers of Jesus refused to attend card parties, nightclubs or even comedy shows. To be a Christian implied a separated life. It is true that there were those who became self-righteous and excessive in their behavior, relying upon the observances of outward rules as a means of appearing to be something they were not inwardly. But most believers felt it was their duty to live in deep consecration to this holy God. They separated themselves from the attractions of this world because they could discern the spirit of the world behind it all and wanted no part of it.

Unfortunately, we do not hear much about holiness these days. In fact, it has been added to today's unspoken list of politically incorrect terms. I believe that the reason people disdain this biblical concept is because they simply don't want such requirements or expectations placed on their lives—not even from the Lord.

Nevertheless, whether or not it is in vogue, the command still sounds out from the sacred pages. Peter said, "As obedient children, do not be conformed to the former lusts which were yours in your ignorance, but like the Holy One who called you, be holy yourselves also in all your behavior; because it is written, 'You shall be holy, for I am holy.'" (1 Peter 1:14-16) This is a commandment, not a request or a suggestion. The book of Hebrews shows the seriousness of this when it states, "Without holiness no one will see the Lord." (Hebrews 12:14 NIV)

The following three quotes about holiness are from writers of yesteryear, when Christians still had a grasp of its importance:

[Holiness] breathes in the prophecy, thunders in the law, murmurs in the narrative, whispers in the promises, supplicates in the prayers, sparkles in the poetry, resounds in the songs, speaks in the types, glows in the imagery, voices in the language, and burns in the spirit of the whole scheme, from the alpha to the omega, from its beginning to its end. Holiness! Holiness needed, holiness required, holiness offered, holiness attainable, holiness a present duty, a present privilege, a present enjoyment, is the progress and completeness of its wondrous theme. It is the truth glowing all over, welling all through revelation—the glorious truth which sparkles and whispers and sings and shouts in all its history, and biography, and poetry, and prophecy, and precept, and promise, and prayer—the great central truth of the system.[4]

The whole design of God was to restore man to his image, and raise him from the ruins of his fall; in a word, to make him perfect; to blot out all his sins, purify his soul, and fill him with all holiness, so that no unholy temper, evil desire, or impure affection or passion shall either lodge or have any being within him. This and this only is true religion, or Christian perfection; and a less salvation than this would be dishonorable to the sacrifice of Christ and the operation of the Holy Ghost.

We must be made partakers of the divine nature. We must be saved from our sins—from the corruption that is in the world, and be holy within and righteous without, or never see God. For this very purpose Jesus Christ lived, died, and revived, that he might purify us unto himself.[5]

The Bible as a whole is a witness for the possibility of holiness. The most careless reader cannot fail to see that it is a Book against sin of every kind and degree.

God has put his whole heart into this work. He designed the great plan of salvation to restore fallen man to holiness. Christ gave himself that he might accomplish this work. The Spirit renews individual believers, and afterwards gives them a sanctifying "baptism of fire," to consume all hidden evil in their hearts, and make them holy....

If the attainability of holiness here... cannot be realized, then Christ was not sincere when he prayed God to "sanctify" us, and put in the lips of all believers a prayer for holiness—"Thy will be done on earth as it is in heaven."[6]

Every person who has the Spirit of Christ living within him will sense a constant prodding toward holiness. Even though there are many teachers who misrepresent grace by inferring it has freed us from God's demand of holiness, the quiet yet strong conviction of the Holy Spirit within a person's heart speaks otherwise. Jesus Christ did not hang on a cross and bleed to death only to have His followers indulge their flesh without concern; He hung there so they could be loosed from the grip of sin and live a life of purity and holiness. The apostle Paul, who championed grace, certainly believed that. He states:

> For this is the will of God, your *sanctification*; that is, that you abstain from sexual immorality; that each of you know how to possess his own vessel in *holiness* and honor, not in lustful passion, like the Gentiles who do not know God; for God has not called us for the purpose of impurity, but in *sanctification*. Consequently, he who rejects this is not rejecting man but the God who gives His Holy Spirit to you. (1 Thessalonians 4:3-8)

God is holy, and He commands His followers to be holy. But what exactly is holiness? The word holy in the Greek is *hagios*, the same word that is translated as "saints." Both usages carry the idea of being consecrated to God and separated from worldliness and sin. When Scripture speaks of holiness, it is referring primarily to a level of consecration and godliness that grows out of obedience and submission to God.

One minister said it this way: "Holiness is properly the name for the state of a soul sanctified wholly, and denotes (1) the absence of depravity, (2) the possession of perfect love. A heart emptied and a heart refilled."[7] Another wrote, "The will is completely adjusted to the will of God and the affections are purified, alienated from sin and the world, and exalted to a supreme love for God."[8] Still another expounded, "True holiness consists of a conformity to the nature and will of God, whereby a saint is distinguished from the unrenewed world, and is not actuated by their principles and precepts, nor governed by their maxims and customs."[9]

The Process of Sanctification

When we mention the word holiness, we are not referring to sinless perfection. However, the believer can and should reach a place in his life where he is no longer controlled by carnal propensities. If Jesus Christ is abiding in a person's heart, it will only be a matter of time before love for God and others will be the prominent passion and driving force of his life.

How do imperfect humans, with their fallen natures, attain to such a high calling? By undergoing the two-fold process of sanctification. The Greek word for "saint" and "holy" (*hagios*) is the root word for sanctify (*hagiazo*). Therefore, the foundational principle of sanctification is *separation unto the Lord*. The resultant holiness is not intrinsic to the believer but results from severing himself from the impurity of *kosmos* and being possessed by a holy God. Sanctification begins with separation.

There are two distinctive acts of sanctification described in Scripture. *Positional sanctification* occurs when a person receives salvation and becomes a saint, a separated one. He is now the "temple of God... that the Spirit of God dwells in" (1 Corinthians 3:16), set apart for the Master's use. He has "been bought with a price" and is no longer his own (1 Corinthians 6:19-20), called by God "unto fellowship with His Son, Jesus Christ our Lord." (1 Corinthians 1:9) All this is done for the new believer by a sovereign act of God and has nothing to do with the level of his spirituality: "And He did so in order that He might make known the riches of His glory upon vessels of mercy, which He prepared beforehand for glory." (Romans 9:23) Positional sanctification has been imputed to a believer through no effort of his own except repentance and faith in Christ. It is the divine designation of one's position as a son of the Most High.

Progressive sanctification describes the development of Christian character. It means to mature in the faith. As the new believer, full of self and all its baggage of sin, pride and selfishness, undergoes the sanctifying processes of God, he gradually conforms to the likeness of Christ. Sanctification is how a person is made holy. It is the *process*; holiness is the *result*.

Paul refers to progressive sanctification when he says that believers are "predestined to become conformed to the image of His Son" (Romans 8:29) and "are being transformed into the same image from glory to glory." (2 Corinthians 3:18) It is what he was referring to when he says, "Do not be conformed to this world, but be transformed by the renewing of your mind." (Romans 12:2) Or in the words of Peter, it involves becoming "partakers of the divine nature, having escaped the corruption that is in the world by lust." (2 Peter 1:4)

Holiness is to the soul what health is to the physical body: freedom from the damaging effects of impurity. Every person is born with a fallen nature, which does not vanish upon salvation. For a Christian to be holy, he must mortify his flesh. (Romans 8:13; Galatians 5:24; Colossians 3:5) He must purify himself. (1 John 3:3) As he struggles against the natural inclinations (lusts) of his flesh, he will become increasingly more like the Lord. The spiritual growth involved in this process is as expected as the physical growth of a child. Stunted growth in either should be considered an aberration.

However, it is important to know that a believer cannot make himself holy. Only the Lord can do that. On the other hand, God will not transform a person who does not long for and strive after holiness. Progressive sanctification requires both the work of the Holy Spirit and the cooperation and effort of the Christian. God will not transform an unwilling heart.

The person must possess a very real longing to be separated from God's enemies (Psalm 139:19-22) and to be filled with His righteousness. (Matthew 5:6)

Cleansing the Vessel

The desire to be like Christ is what motivates a believer to separate himself from the world. Alexander McLaren rightly said, "The measure of our discord with the world is the measure of our accord with Christ."[10]

I need to make it clear that separating oneself from the world does not necessarily bring a person into holiness. It puts the believer into a position of being made holy, but it in itself does not create holiness. Most of us have seen or heard of those whose whole relationship with God seems to revolve around their ability to remain separated from this world system. There are certain groups in the U.S. today where the men drive buggies and the women maintain their homes without the aid of electricity. I personally appreciate the uncluttered lifestyle such people have chosen to live. Most I have spoken to have a refreshing innocence about them that many of us city-dwellers and suburbanites lack. However, refraining from driving a car does not make one holy. Andrew Murray correctly observes, "Though there can be no holiness without separation, there can be separation that does not lead to holiness."[11]

What a conscious severing of ourselves from the world should do, however, is to make us receptive to the sanctifying work of the Holy Spirit. No one sets a drinking glass on the counter for people to admire. A glass has a practical purpose: to hold a beverage. Borrowing Paul's illustration: "Now in a large house there are not only gold and silver vessels, but also vessels of wood and of earthenware, and some to honor and some to dishonor. Therefore, if a man cleanses himself from these things, he will be a vessel for honor, sanctified, useful to the Master, prepared for every good work. Now flee from youthful lusts, and pursue righteousness, faith, love and peace, with those who call on the Lord from a pure heart." (2 Timothy 2:20-22)

Until the vessel has been emptied and cleansed, it will remain unusable. The same is true in our lives. As long as we are full of the things of this world, we will not be filled with the Holy Spirit. Until we renounce our love for the things of the world, God will view our claims of love for Him as nothing more than empty chatter. (1 John 2:15) These two competing loves cannot occupy the same heart.

The Lord's desire for us, just as it was for ancient Israel, is to make us dispensers of His knowledge to a fallen world. He wants to live out His holy life through us. He cannot do this if we remain attached to willful sin and misplaced affections. Andrew Murray, who obeyed God by remaining in a small country parish in South Africa rather than accepting a call to one of the most prestigious churches in London, said the following about the process of sanctification:

> It is as God gets and takes full possession of us, as the eternal life in Christ has the mastery of our whole being, as the Holy Spirit flows fully and freely through us, so that we dwell in God, and God in us, that separation will be, not a thing of ordinances and observances, but a spiritual reality....
>
> It is the consciousness of God's Indwelling Presence, making and keeping us His very own, that works the true separateness from the world and its spirit, from our own will and ourselves. And it is as this separation is accepted and prized and persevered in by us, that the holiness of God will enter in and take possession. He separates us for Himself, and sanctifies us to be His dwelling. He comes Himself to take personal possession by the indwelling of Christ in the heart. And we are then truly separate, and kept separate, by the presence of God within us.[12]

Be Holy As I Am Holy

Steps to Holiness

Time and age alone do not produce holiness; neither does a vague faith that God will sanctify us "if and when He chooses." Nor does He arbitrarily select some for perfection while leaving others in an unholy state. The doorway to holiness is open to all. The depth of our consecration has much to do with our hunger for righteousness and our willingness to struggle against sin. Spiritual lethargy hinders the pursuit of holiness. Eating life's "junk food" leaves us with no hunger for holiness. Lust and covetousness are the enemies of a thirst for purity. The life of holiness is available to those who are willing to do battle against the world, the flesh, and the devil.

The one who enters this narrow path learns quickly that his greatest enemy is his own flesh. Only through deep and persistent repentance will his sinful habit patterns be overcome. I will give a personal example to illustrate this point.

Some years ago, my in-laws visited us from California. One day, my wife and I took them to Cincinnati. We happened to pass a store we had shopped at years before during one of their previous visits. As we were reminiscing about that store, I remembered an incident that occurred while we were shopping there when I had spoken rudely to my mother-in-law. Even though she had graciously "forgiven and forgotten," I never forgot it. As I reminded her of that incident, my wife asked me if I had repented of it. "About a million times," I responded.

My mother-in-law kindly said, "Steve, you only needed to repent once."

"It isn't repentance if I keep doing the same thing to other people," I replied.

As far as my standing with her and God is concerned, it is true I needed to ask her forgiveness only once. But in those days I had a sharp tongue, which could be sarcastic and ugly.

What was worse was that I couldn't seem to control it. Yes, I was forgiven for my actions, but I wanted a deeper repentance. I wanted to change.

Incidents similar to that one would play over and over in my mind. I grieved over the way I would talk to others at times. I sought God for a greater love for others, a softer tongue, a gentler disposition. And He answered those prayers! The transformation came gradually; the ugly incidents occurred less often, with less intensity.

God alone gets the glory for changing me, but it took repeated times of repentance and serious battles against my natural inclinations on my part to pave the way for Him to accomplish that inward transformation. The Lord is willing to change anyone who truly wants to change.

Of course, overcoming habitual sin is only one aspect of the process of sanctification. God's grace encompasses ALL of our needs, even when we are unaware of areas where the divine scalpel must do its cutting work. The roots of selfishness and pride go very deep and we may sometimes wonder if a lifetime is long enough for the work of God to be completed in us! But the more we yield, the more He will accomplish His purpose to conform us to the image of Christ.

THE NECESSITY OF HOLY LIVING

One of the greatest misunderstandings I have seen amongst Christians is the unspoken notion that a person can live a selfish, worldly life on earth and then somehow magically be transformed through the process of death into a holy, God-loving saint. The truth is that the eternal realm is only a continuation of a person's life on earth. The inward life, the character, the soul of a person continues on in perpetuity forever. So will the ruling loves of one's heart. In fact, I think Scripture is fairly clear that a person's object of affection (whether it be God or some idol) will determine a person's eternal residence. As Jesus said, "Where your treasure is, there your heart will be also." (Matthew 6:21)

In the last chapter, I touched upon the idea that heaven would be a miserable place for God's enemies. I find that I must revisit this subject to emphasize this extremely important point. Once again I must turn to the inspired words of the writers of yesteryear to properly articulate this truth.

> There is no [idea] so pernicious as this—that persons not purified, not sanctified, not made holy in their life, should afterwards be taken into that state of blessedness which consists in the enjoyment of God. Neither can such persons enjoy God, nor would God be a reward to them. Holiness indeed is perfected in heaven: but the beginning of it is invariably confined to this world.[13]

How shall we ever be at home and happy in heaven, if we die unholy? Death works no change. The grave makes no alteration. Each will rise again with the same character in which he breathed his last. Where will our place be if we are strangers to holiness now?

Suppose for a moment that you were allowed to enter heaven without holiness. What would you do? What possible enjoyment could you feel there? To which of all the saints would you join yourself? Their pleasures are not your pleasures, their tastes not your tastes, their character not your character. How could you possibly be happy, if you had not been holy on earth?

Now perhaps you love the company of the light and the careless, the worldly-minded and the covetous, the reveler and the pleasure-seeker. There will be none such in heaven.

Now perhaps you think the saints of God too strict and serious. You rather avoid them....There will be no other company in heaven.

Think you that such an one would delight to meet David, and Paul, and John, after a life spent in doing the very things they spoke against?

People may say, in a vague way, "they hope to go to heaven;" but they do not consider what they say....Heaven is essentially a holy place; its inhabitants are all holy; its occupations are all holy. It is clear and plain that we must be somewhat trained and made ready for heaven while we are on earth.[14]

Given the Bible's overwhelming emphasis on our need for holiness, why is it mentioned so rarely from our pulpits today? Perhaps it is because subtle alterations have been introduced into the Church which have brought about a gradual change in priorities. If there truly is some kind of a Satanic conspiracy to deceive people away from holy living and true Christianity, it would only make sense that part of the plan would be to create a false system of evangelical Christianity that would lull people into an unfounded sense of security. Certainly the condition of the Body of Christ today is a clear indication that things are not as they should be.

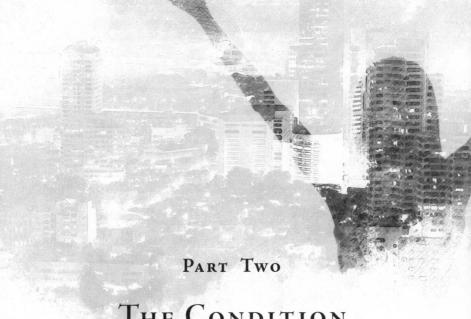

PART TWO

THE CONDITION
OF THE CHURCH

"My concern is the measure of infiltration by the
world into the church. We have been influenced far
more than we would like to admit. This infiltration
has dulled our effectivenes, blurred our vision, and
caused us to adopt worldly standards of success."

-Billy Melvin

"I am absolutely convinced that meaninglessness does not come from being weary of pain. Meaninglessness comes from being weary of pleasure. And that's why we are bankrupt of meaning in a land of so much."[1]

-Ravi Zacharias

"The Kingdom of Babylon is often willing to acknowledge God; it is just not willing to submit to Him or admit its need for Him. What is the ultimate goal of the kingdom of Babylon? I believe its seductive mannerisms, overshadowing power, and intermingled nature is designed to ultimately lead to complete and absolute *domination*."[2]

-Steve Harrison

6

THE CHURCH
OF LAODICEA

We return to the island of Patmos. As John lay at the feet of the Transfigured Savior, Jesus began speaking to him. In the moments that followed, the Lord delivered seven of the purest messages any human could ever hope to hear. Seven churches were addressed in what eventually became the 51 verses of Revelation 2 and 3. John probably had visited all of those churches in Asia Minor, including the congregation at Laodicea. He undoubtedly knew the pastor and many of the church members there personally. But no sentimental memory of the people blocked him from sending to them the exact words Jesus spoke about their spiritual condition.

Many scholars believe that these seven churches represent the history of the Christian Church. If that is true, the word given to Laodicea is an extremely important message for believers today. The correlation between the Laodicean Church and the American Church (along with its dominating worldwide presence) cannot be missed.

There is no question we in the American Church are enjoying our finest hour. Never in the history of Christianity have there been so many conversions, so many churches, and so much money to support the evangelical enterprise. Church buildings have never been bigger. Services have never been so packed. Christian movies and Christian music are big business. Christianity permeates every facet of American life. We have Christian baseball stars, Christian politicians, Christian actors, Christian millionaires, and we even had a Christian heavyweight boxing champ!

Christianity is flourishing, not just in America, but also around the world. The Gospel is available to the entire world via satellite. The Word is preached on television twenty-four hours a day. Christian radio virtually blankets the planet. Well-supplied missionaries are taking the Gospel to nearly every country and ethnic group on earth.

Brilliant people in key positions who believe in what they are doing have dedicated themselves and their abilities to the spreading of the Gospel. They work tirelessly and efficiently to promote the cause. Strategists have laid out a battle plan for winning the world for Christ, and it is working! Fresh ideas are flowing. Seeker-friendly churches have opened their doors to the wary and cynical. Christian psychologists are bringing modern credibility to a Church tired of combating the old stereotype of uneducated "Bible thumpers." Soul winners present a positive message about God's blessings for His children. Christian rock bands make discipleship noisy and fun.

Everywhere we turn in the field of ministry, we find bank accounts bulging, numbers increasing, organizations expanding, denominations flourishing, and new converts multiplying. Surely, things could not look better for the Bride of Jesus Christ than they do today! All that remains to happen is the Rapture, so we can all go home to a well-deserved reward and leave the rest of the world to fend for itself during the Great Tribulation.

The Church of Laodicea

It was much the same in the Laodicean fellowship at the end of the first century. That church was probably pastored by Archippus, the son of the rich merchant, Philemon. (Philemon 1:2) The members of the congregation were content. Everything was at peace. The future looked promising for these Christians, who were able to keep the faith while maintaining a comfortable lifestyle.

I have stood in the ruins of Laodicea and can understand why they were so confident. Situated between the small village of Colossae and the resort town of Hieropolis, Laodicea was the commercial center of a rich, fertile valley. It had a beautiful Greek amphitheater, an enormous Roman coliseum, and many other magnificent structures that bespoke its prosperity. Since the church in Laodicea was not under any persecution, everything was going well for this body of believers.

By comparison, the little congregations in Smyrna and Philadelphia must have looked pathetic to the high-flying members of the Laodicean flock! The saints of Smyrna, known for their poverty and deprivation, obviously were not enjoying "God's blessings." The chief characteristic of the flock in Philadelphia was its lack of power. No doubt, their ministers were short on charisma and colorful, entertaining preaching. To the saints in Laodicea, the congregations in Philadelphia and Smyrna were dwindling and dying, unable to relate and be relevant. By all outward appearances, they were both miserable failures.

And yet, when "the faithful and true Witness" spoke, He only had praise for them. Surely there must be some mistake here! How could it be possible that Jesus would have nothing good to say about the thriving assembly in Laodicea and only commendation for the downtrodden believers of Smyrna and Philadelphia?

As I have prayed and wept over Christ's message to the Laodiceans and how it applies to the Last-Days-Laodicean Church of America, several things stand out to me.

The first was the obvious discrepancy between Jesus' assessment of their condition and their own view of it. The Laodiceans viewed their pathetic condition in a completely positive light, oblivious of their true state. We can almost hear the bounding happiness in their voices as they boasted, "We are rich and wealthy and have need of nothing!" The unspoken inference was, "God is blessing!" This upbeat mindset must have been constantly reinforced through the success they were enjoying individually and as a fellowship. They probably considered their "positive mental attitude" to be faith. They were happy and things were indeed going well for them. They were not interested in "negative preaching." In the midst of their peace and prosperity the last thing they wanted to hear was a message of "gloom and doom." Had Timothy, Iraneus, or Polycarp—all saintly men of that era—preached repentance in Laodicea, they would have been quickly judged as being too legalistic or harsh.

But Jesus told the Laodiceans something they did "not know." Jesus, the Omniscient One, saw things differently than they. His response to their delusion was, "You say, 'I am rich, and have become wealthy, and have need of nothing' and you do not know that you are wretched and miserable and poor and blind and naked." (Revelation 3:17) In His mercy He exposed them. They never grasped the significance of what He had taught years before: "Not even when one has an abundance does his life consist of his possessions." (Luke 12:15)

Notice how differently Jesus spoke to the feeble saints of Smyrna, whom He called "rich" in the midst of their poverty, and to those of Philadelphia, whom He commended for their faithfulness in the midst of persecution. These seasoned saints could have taught their prosperous brothers in Laodicea something about real Christianity. True, they had little outward success. It is unlikely that they had people flocking to their services. Their assemblies probably amounted to nothing more than a small handful who met in homes. Yet, these dear people were "rich toward God," while the Laodiceans were "wretched and miserable and poor and blind and naked."

A worldly church views success differently than Jesus views it. The former sees *outward* success and its trappings—large buildings, lucrative bank accounts, and hordes of idolizing followers. The latter sees the narrow path to the Cross and the *inward* qualities of a godly life, humility, and a real devotion to meeting the needs of others.

Prosperity tends to blind a person to his spiritual impoverishment and creates a false sense of wellbeing and eternal security. When the Laodiceans examined themselves, they saw only divine favor and blessings, leaving them with an attitude that they were "in need of nothing." Everything seemed good because troubles were absent. It was easy to be a follower of Christ. Things were running smoothly, there was plenty of everything, and opposition was non-existent.

Jesus prescribed eye salve (truth) to cure their blindness. The truth could reveal how spiritually nearsighted they were. It would show them their obvious lack of reverence for God and how closely they were allied with the enemy. Through eyes of truth they would see the needs of others and the passion of Christ to help them.

Of the Laodicean condition Jesus said, "I know your deeds, that you are neither cold nor hot; I would that you were cold or hot. So because you are lukewarm, and neither hot nor cold, I will spit you out of My mouth." (Revelation 3:15-16) Back and forth the Laodiceans would go, first in love with Jesus and then in love with the world. One gets the definite sense that Jesus would prefer they would go one way or the other. Such compromising faith is neither the ice-cold existence of one who doesn't know God nor the fervent passion of one who truly loves Him. The Laodicean believers did not oppose the Gospel, yet they did not fully embrace it. They were not committing flagrant sin, but they were not striving for holiness. They were not mockers, and yet they moderated their enthusiasm lest it be misconstrued as fanaticism. They did everything properly so no one would be offended, especially the unsaved who were being groomed for membership. They had their successful programs, but they had no godly power.

THE AMERICAN EVANGELICAL ETHOS

How comparable is the 21st Century Church with this thriving congregation! We too have created a gospel for our own culture, tailor-made to fit smugly within the confines of the American Dream. The old-fashioned Gospel we should preach has been altered just enough to agree with our busy schedules and myriad amusements. By emphasizing certain biblical teachings and, more importantly, neglecting others, we have managed to create a whole new gospel that fits our American lifestyle.

Tragically, our rendition of Christianity makes no demands, expects no sacrifice, and yields no eternal rewards. The Lion of Judah has been anesthetized, declawed, and tamed. In the midst of our busy lives, we have reduced the Almighty to a harmless icon to whom we pay superficial homage. The vision of a Holy God, a Consuming Fire, a Judge who will one day render unto every man his just reward has virtually vanished out of the American Church. We have inoculated Christianity to such a degree that we treat God as though He were our aging family dog whom we let into the Church once a week, pat on the head, and send back into the yard with a bone to chew on. We may render Him patronizing compliments occasionally for conscience' sake, but there's no substance to our words because we don't really mean them. We sing songs of praise but hardly get beyond emotion to the significance of them. We cling to a form of godliness, but there is no power. We honor Him with our mouths, but our hearts are far from Him. Woe to the inhabitants of this Church generation!

Furthermore, we have heaped to ourselves a host of preachers who tickle our ears with nuggets of biblical truth that satisfy information-crazed saintlings without ever stepping on toes or confronting sin. What is preached is not wrong, *per se*. It simply is an incomplete Gospel. The parts that make people uncomfortable are avoided, and destructive blows to sin are never rendered.

Pastors who do call on believers to live holy lives are so black and blue from sheep bites they hardly have the strength to press on. Many have given up the fight and retreated into secular employment. Others have acquiesced and joined the ranks with those who feed an already emaciated flock with sermons lacking real substance or depth.

The more we elevate "ear-tickling" preachers into superstars, the more we become convinced of how right we are. Every new personality who doesn't preach against sin, carnality, and worldliness deepens our delusion. How could so many be off the mark? Is it because we believe what we want to believe and hear what we want to hear? If a godly preacher tries to bring things into balance, he is quickly labeled, of all things, as being "unbalanced!"

We are being fed a steady, unwholesome diet of spiritual mush in America. We have been handed substitutes for so long we have forgotten what real meat tastes like. This dilution of spiritual truth has been so gradual it has gone undetected even by those who are supposed to be spiritually discerning. Now, there are scarcely any traces of real substance left at all. I wish someone would stand up and yell like the old lady in the 1984 Wendy's commercial, "Where's the beef?!"

Leonard Ravenhill rightly said, "The church has been subnormal for so long that when it finally becomes normal, everybody will think it's abnormal."[3] Or as Watchman Nee put it, "By the time the average Christian gets his temperature up to normal, everybody thinks he's got a fever."[4] It's not that every believer is this way, but the lowered standard is now the accepted norm in America.

American Christians have become so satisfied with a substitute gospel that they no longer hunger for the real thing. We eat just enough junk food to keep ourselves from getting hungry. With no hunger pangs, we never feel our need for real spiritual food. We're starving and don't seem to care. In our minds, we're satisfied and have need of nothing. And who is responsible for creating and marketing the spiritual junk food? That's right, the devil, also known as *kosmos*, who will do anything to keep us from seeing our need for solid food.

America is in the same crisis as the Laodicean believers. Prosperity has weakened our daily dependence upon God. Instead of asking, "How can I rid myself of the poisonous influences of this world?" we ask, "How much of this world can I have and still go to heaven?" A lady who lived this Laodicean "Christianity" and was active in an evangelical church for years gave the following testimony during a revival meeting I attended. I won't comment on her theology but simply let her testimony speak for itself.

Twenty-two years ago I got saved, filled with the Spirit, and water baptized. I joined a Spirit-filled church, but my husband and I fell into a religious trap. We went to church every time the doors were open. We had every position and title in the church you can imagine. At one time he was the administrator of a Bible college. We were deacons, Sunday school teachers, and altar workers. We counseled people and taught the newcomers class; you name it, and we did it.

We sang praise, worshiped, and said shallow prayers, but during the week we lived the way we wanted to. We thought because we didn't drink, smoke, or party that we were going to heaven. We fell into the lie that most of the churches are feeding in America today. It is a lie; do not believe it. We were miserable and disappointed in Christianity. In fact, we were disappointed in God because that's what we thought Christianity was all about. There was no power whatsoever.

When our daughter left home in November, we were devastated. We talked about coming to the revival, but we just felt it was for the unsaved. We didn't feel it was for us, but we thought maybe we might glean something from it. We drove here on a Wednesday and sat in the back of the sanctuary. Steve Hill gave an altar call.

As I sat there I remember that my heart wasn't beating. There was no conviction. That's how lost I was. Sometimes we who have been in the Church for years—especially those of us who have been in leadership—are the hardest people to reach, because we don't feel that we have that need. We really feel that we are saved. Sometimes the alcoholic is easier to preach to because he knows he has a need. It's the religious people in the Church that are blind who don't feel that they have need. It's that Pharisee, hypocrisy spirit. As I sat there watching all the people come to the altar I thought, "Isn't that sweet. God bless them; they're getting saved."

I went to sleep that night and got up the next morning to brush my teeth. As I stood there in front of the mirror, in my self-righteous, pious way I said, "Oh Lord, just give me more of You."

He said, "No! I want more of you!" I began to break and everything Brother Hill said the night before began to haunt me. It was Thanksgiving Day. I was so miserable that day I couldn't even go out to eat. We came to the service that night, and the Lord began to show me what I was like. I was lukewarm, deceived, and a stench in His nostrils.

As I thought about going to the altar, I remembered that there were people from my church in the sanctuary. I thought I would just slip up the side aisle and repent. He said, "Oh no you don't! You've been playing the game and discreetly slipping in and out for twenty-two years. If you want these religious shackles removed from your life, you run up that center aisle in front of everybody. You need to break that pride. No more religion!" I ran up that aisle and threw myself down at the altar and asked God to forgive me.

EYES OF LOVE

Those same love-filled eyes that saw into the pitiable inner condition of that couple in 1997 saw into the heart of a prosperous young man in 31 A. D. who ran to Jesus to inquire how he could have eternal life. Jesus answered him by saying,

> "You know the commandments, 'Do not murder, do not commit adultery, do not steal, do not bear false witness, do not defraud, honor your father and mother.'"
>
> And he said to Him, "Teacher, I have kept all these things from my youth up."
>
> And looking at him, Jesus felt a love for him, and said to him, "One thing you lack: go and sell all you possess, and give to the poor, and you shall have treasure in heaven; and come, follow Me."
>
> But at these words his face fell, and he went away grieved, for he was one who owned much property. And Jesus, looking around, said to His disciples, "How hard it will be for those who are wealthy to enter the kingdom of God!" (Mark 10:19-23)

This young ruler had kept the outward requirements of religion. If his story were updated for today we would find him serving as a board member in a local church, keeping up appearances. He would be in services every week, faithfully tithing. Drinking, cussing, or womanizing would be out of the question. He would be a good man in the eyes of his neighbors and successful at work. But something would be missing that Jesus' piercing gaze could detect. Rex Andrews comments on this story:

> Oh the Love flowing forth, from the soon-to-be-offered Lamb of God, as He looked upon the one who had been touched by His Word! How willingly and in what utter consecration Jesus was heading toward The Cross! With what single-eyed determination was His face set toward The Jerusalem which killed the messengers which God had sent! And with what unutterable tenderness and encompassing compassion did He say: You lack One Thing. Go sell everything you own, and give it away to the needy, and treasure will be yours in the heavens. Then come, TAKE UP YOUR CROSS and follow me. And the bright and urgent interest faded out of the seeker's countenance. He became sad—at God's WORD—and went away grieved.
>
> What was the grief which had descended upon him? Simply the "love of this world," and attachment to its possessions. That desolating world-love could give up eternal life; and give up The Jesus who loved; and turn away to his world-wedded earth life when The Cross loomed up before him. A decision was made, by which Jesus declared the awfulness of the POWER of the love of this world and its worthless riches.[5]

Not long before this incident took place, Jesus described the failure of some professing believers: "The worry of the world, and the deceitfulness of riches choke the word, and it becomes unfruitful." (Matthew 13:22) This was a pronouncement of spiritual fact. The "deceitfulness of riches" warps a person's discernment to the point that he believes he is living for God, when in reality he is living for the things of the world. These words are reminiscent of some other statements Jesus made about the lack of fruit: "Every tree that does not bear good fruit is cut down and thrown into the fire." (Matthew 7:19) "Every branch in Me that does not bear fruit, He takes away.... He is thrown away as a branch, and dries up; and they gather them, and cast them into the fire, and they are burned." (John 15:2-6)

Prosperity makes the human heart highly susceptible to deception. The Laodiceans saw themselves as spiritual; they weren't in need from a materialistic standpoint. And herein lies the danger to you, the reader, right now: the same power of deception that leads people into compromise *is the same power which would cause you to quickly dismiss the message of this chapter.* Are you a Laodicean Christian?

The Pearl of Great Price is standing at the door knocking, asking us to "sell all" that we might have Him. The "all" for us is simply the things of the world that have choked out our love for Him. Those eyes of love are looking at you right now, dear reader. His voice is pleading with you. "Will you divorce yourself from the things of this world which are keeping you from Me and follow Me with your whole heart?"

The rich young ruler walked away from those eyes and that voice, unwilling to say "Yes" to the Lord. The Laodiceans, equally unwilling, were less honest with themselves, but their delusion did not alter the reality of their rejection of Christ. Their church had been in existence some forty years at that point. Now they were wavering between Jesus and Babylon. The Jesus who loved them spoke truthfully, like a spurned lover making one last appeal. The half-hearted church could vacillate no longer. Their time to choose had come. Either they would answer His knock and open the door, or He would vomit them out.

We *can* find our way back to our first love, but we must start with an honest evaluation of our spiritual condition. We can no longer put off the appraisal. Today is the day, and now is the time, for *confession* and *repentance*. May the cry of our hearts continue to be, "Search me, O God, and know my heart; try me and know my anxious thoughts; and see if there be any hurtful way in me, and lead me in the everlasting way." (Psalm 139:23-24)

"As much as God desires the salvation of men, He will not prostitute heaven, and set the gates of it wide open to those who only fly to it in extremity but never sought it in good earnest, nor indeed do now care for it, or desire it for any other reason, but to excuse them from going to hell."[1]

-Richard Baxter

"Do you love nobody? Do you live within yourself? Are you immured within your own ribs? Is self all your world? Then you will go to hell. There is no help for it; for the place of unloving spirits is the bottomless pit. Only he that loves can live in heaven, for heaven is love: and you cannot go to glory unless you have learned to love, and to find it your very life to do good to those about you."[2]

-C.H. Spurgeon

7

You Need
Not Obey God

Despite the smothering cloud of deception and delusion saturating the spiritual atmosphere, an urgent call is ringing out over America from a remnant of sober and godly saints. They are not a part of any particular denomination or movement *per se*. They are simply holy men and women who live consecrated lives and know what it means to pray. It might be a preacher who has been relegated to some insignificant pastorate in a small town. It could be a grandmother who weeps in intercession every morning. Or perhaps it is a housewife who lives a sanctified lifestyle despite heavy criticism. Discerning saints with ears turned to God are relaying the same message: "Come Out! Be holy as I am holy!" How I wish every believer would welcome such a refreshing call to repentance and holiness!

Tragically, there is another cry so deafening that hardly anyone can hear what God is saying to those "with ears to hear." That ungodly voice shouts out, "You don't have to be holy!" Entire denominations and church movements teach that a person does not really have to obey God. This false message is loudly proclaimed from pulpits, over Christian radio, and through a barrage of books aimed at giving churchgoers a false sense of security. Its vocal proponents shout down anyone who counters it. "You're teaching legalism! You're telling people they have to earn their way to heaven! There is nothing a person can do to save himself. It's all God's grace!"

With most deceptions, there is usually enough truth embedded in the message to make it believable. And it should be acknowledged that a strongly legalistic presentation of Christianity lends itself to a "saved by works" understanding of the Gospel. But there isn't enough of that unbalanced teaching in church circles to warrant the overwhelming emphasis on grace that Christendom has heard in the last 20-30 years. One would think that legalism is the greatest threat the Church has ever faced, considering the inundation of teachings given on grace. The truth of the matter is that the real threat is from those teachings which have, in the name of Grace, encouraged believers to indulge themselves in a selfish and worldly lifestyle, far from the abundant life Jesus had in mind for His Bride.

No doubt Satan in his subtlety has planned every aspect of this strategy for the last days. An outright statement that "sinning doesn't matter" would be too strong a poison for believers to swallow. Satan instead concocted an entire doctrinal scheme that would allow for such worldly living. By leading Bible teachers to over-emphasize God's grace and de-emphasize the need for godliness and holiness, the devil has made compromised living acceptable in the eyes of the average churchgoer. Through the concerted efforts of many false teachers, holiness is now politically incorrect and licentiousness the status quo.

A WARNING TO END-TIME BELIEVERS

Paul gave an extremely important clue about what to expect in the last days when he said, "For the time will come when they will not endure sound doctrine; but wanting to have their ears tickled, they will accumulate for themselves teachers in accordance to their own desires; and will turn away their ears from the truth, and will turn aside to myths." (2 Timothy 4:3-4) Could he be referring to the Church today? Certainly!* The reality of it is in full bloom, right before our eyes today. "The time" not only "*will* come;" it *has* come!

This Greek word for desire, *epithumia*, is the same word we find in our theme passage of 1 John 2:16, "the *lust* of the flesh and the *lust* of the eyes.... And the world is passing away, and also its *lusts*." In other words, Paul was saying: "In the last days people will exalt teachers who offer a form of Christianity that allows people to live for the desires of their flesh. In essence, they will drift away from real Christianity and will refuse to listen to the truth."

Today, the great emphasis on grace without real *sanctification* is exactly what Paul warned against. What could possibly be more ungodly than teaching people that they can love this world, remain in sin and still go to heaven?

Many of those who thus argue in support of unrighteousness do so in part because they live such carnal, worldly lifestyles themselves and have no conviction about the despicable nature of sin. In their minds, crossing the will of a holy God is not something to be overly concerned about. They are the ones Paul spoke of when he said, "For God has not called us for the purpose of impurity, but in sanctification. So, he who rejects this is not rejecting man but the God who gives His Holy Spirit to you." (1 Thessalonians 4:7-8) Warnings like this are of no concern to these false teachers, however. They are fully confident they are right, even though Scripture clearly contradicts their teachings and basic ideologies. Unfortunately, these men have risen to occupy some of the most influential positions in the end-time Church. Their message is so compelling and embraced with such enthusiasm that it becomes nearly

---

* The context preceding this statement is what this world will be like in the last days.

impossible for anyone to stand against it. Nevertheless, the truth of God's Word and His counsel stands forever.

THE PROOF OF FAITH

James, the half-brother of Jesus and the leader of the church in Jerusalem, was known by all to be a very pious man. His epistle has a down-to-earth quality. In it he defines true religion. "This is pure and undefiled religion in the sight of our God and Father, to visit orphans and widows in their distress, and to keep oneself unstained by the world." (James 1:27) The life of the true believer will be characterized by these two hallmarks of true Christianity. First, living out God's love to those in need; second, a pure life lived out in a polluted world. James then went on to give a practical definition of saving faith and a definitive teaching on what it *does*.

> For judgment will be merciless to one who has shown no mercy; mercy triumphs over judgment. What use is it, my brethren, if a man says he has faith, but he has no works? Can that faith save him? If a brother or sister is without clothing and in need of daily food, and one of you says to them, "Go in peace, be warmed and be filled," and yet you do not give them what is necessary for their body, what use is that?
>
> Even so faith, if it has no works, is dead, being by itself. But someone may well say, "You have faith, and I have works; show me your faith without the works, and I will show you my faith by my works." You believe that God is one. You do well; the demons also believe, and shudder. But are you willing to recognize, you foolish fellow, that faith without works is useless? (James 2:13-20)

At first glance, one might think that James was refuting the teachings of the apostle Paul who continually asserted that a person is not saved by works but by faith. However, a closer examination of the subject shows that there really is no contradiction here. Matthew Henry explains this passage of Scripture:

> When Paul says that *a man is justified by faith, without the deeds of the law* (Romans 3:28), he plainly speaks of another sort of work than James does, but not of another sort of faith. Paul speaks of works wrought in obedience to the law of Moses, and before men's embracing the faith of the gospel; and he had to deal with those who valued themselves so highly upon those works that they rejected the gospel (as Romans 10, at the beginning most expressly declares); but James speaks of works done in obedience to the gospel, and as the proper and necessary effects and fruits of sound believing in Christ Jesus. Both are concerned to magnify the faith of the gospel, as that which alone could save us and justify us; but Paul magnifies it by showing the insufficiency of any works of the law before faith, or in opposition to the doctrine of justification by Jesus Christ; James magnifies the same faith, by showing what are the genuine and necessary products and operations of it....It is by *faith* only that we are put into a justified state, but then good works come in for the completing of our justification at the last great day; then, *Come you children of my Father —for I was hungry, and you gave me meat, etc.*[3]

One is not saved by works. Salvation results from the combination of God's grace and a person's faith. (Ephesians 2:8) However, those who think that they can do whatever they please after their "conversion" should consider these biblical statements: Jesus said, "For the Son of Man is going to come in the glory of His Father with His angels; and will then recompense every man according to his *deeds*." (Matthew 16:27) He also said that "those who did the *good deeds* [would be destined] to a resurrection of life, those who committed the *evil deeds* to a resurrection of judgment." (John 5:29)

Paul, writing to members of the church in Rome, said the following:

> Or do you think lightly of the riches of His kindness and forbearance and patience, not knowing that the kindness of God leads you to repentance? But because of your stubbornness and unrepentant heart you are storing up wrath for yourself in the day of wrath and revelation of the righteous judgment of God, who will render to every man according to his *deeds*: to those who by perseverance in *doing good* seek for glory and honor and immortality, eternal life; but to those who are selfishly ambitious and *do not obey the truth*, but obey unrighteousness, wrath and indignation. (Romans 2:4-8)

So we see that what one does in life directly affects one's eternal destiny. It is true, one is saved by faith alone; and yet, there is a quality in the life of a person with *saving faith* that manifests itself by the works he does. Let's look at three such indicators.

The first and most obvious proof of conversion is continual growth in obedience to God. His life is characterized by an ongoing process of spiritual growth. Through recurrent periods of brokenness and God's discipline, the old self-centered life, with its pride and wickedness, is overcome and the fruit of the Spirit begins to appear. This is the process of sanctification, "without which no one will see the Lord." (Hebrews 12:14)[†]

---

† A fatal mistake made by many is to think that learning about Christianity by hearing sermons and reading books is the same as sanctification. Hearing is important, but for good reason James told believers to "prove yourselves doers of the word, and not merely hearers who delude themselves." (James 1:22)

A second proof of a genuine conversion is the development of an eternal perspective. Eternity is always in the back of the genuine believer's mind. He understands and lives by the words of Jesus: "He who loves his life loses it; and he who hates his life in this world shall keep it to life eternal." (John 12:25) Because he has an eternal perspective, he lives as an alien in a foreign land. The world is not his home but a temporary stopping place. His rewards are not to be achieved on this earth but in heaven. He loves Jesus' words: "Do not lay up for yourselves treasures upon earth, where moth and rust destroy, and where thieves break in and steal. But lay up for yourselves treasures in heaven, where neither moth nor rust destroys, and where thieves do not break in or steal." (Matthew 6:19-20) The primary focus of his life is not to achieve what the world offers but what awaits him in eternity.

The final characteristic of an authentic conversion is expressed in the words of Jesus: "By this all men will know that you are My disciples, if you have love for one another." (John 13:35) The apostle John elaborated on this more fully.

> By this the children of God and the children of the devil are obvious: anyone who does not practice righteousness is not of God, nor the one who does not love his brother. For this is the message which you have heard from the beginning, that we should love one another....
>
> We know that we have passed out of death into life, because we love the brethren. He who does not love abides in death....
>
> We know love by this, that He laid down His life for us; and we ought to lay down our lives for the brethren. But whoever has the world's goods, and beholds his brother in need and closes his heart against him, how does the love of God abide in him? (1 John 3:10, 14, 16-18)

John wrote this passage of Scripture to help sincere God-seekers to know whether or not they had truly been regenerated. The person with a real desire to "know" whether he has "passed out of death into life" will be able to tell by his love for "the brethren." God's love flowing through a person's life is the one sure sign that there is a true, living faith behind it. Likewise, the absence of it should be cause for the most urgent concern.[‡]

DEAD FAITH

Every Sunday morning in American churches thousands of believers sing with great emotion about their passionate love and commitment to God. What frightens me is the extent of delusion involved in that. "Christians don't tell lies," Peter Marshall said, "they just sing them." Many people sit in church who have never truly surrendered their lives to the Lord; they have never really put their faith in Him. They can get by through the selective obedience of "cafeteria Christianity": picking and choosing what "rules" they can live with. They lack the resurrection life of a transformed heart. Paul warned that in the last days many who claimed to be followers of Christ would in fact be "lovers of pleasure rather than lovers of God, holding to a form of godliness, although they have denied its power." (2 Timothy 3:4-5) There is no power because there is no submission.

The Pharisees were extreme examples of this. Their outward actions expressed strict obedience to the commandments of the Law, but inwardly something was very wrong; their hearts were far from God, as Jesus told them.

Woe to you, scribes and Pharisees, hypocrites! For you tithe mint and dill and cummin, and have neglected the

---

‡ If one does not see these principles at work in his life, the answer is not to try to go out and do them; that would be attempting to save oneself by works. The answer is to start crying out to God in real repentance. The Lord will answer that prayer and supply all that is lacking.

weightier provisions of the law: justice and mercy and faithfulness; but these are the things you should have done without neglecting the others. You blind guides, who strain out a gnat and swallow a camel!

Woe to you, scribes and Pharisees, hypocrites! For you clean the outside of the cup and of the dish, but inside they are full of robbery and self-indulgence. You blind Pharisee, first clean the inside of the cup and of the dish, so that the outside of it may become clean also.

Woe to you, scribes and Pharisees, hypocrites! For you are like whitewashed tombs which on the outside appear beautiful, but inside they are full of dead men's bones and all uncleanness. Even so you too outwardly appear righteous to men, but inwardly you are full of hypocrisy and lawlessness. (Matthew 23:23-28)

These words are of extreme importance to believers today because *they reveal the danger of living by outward standards without having a true change of heart.* These religious leaders scrupulously obeyed the biblical commandments that governed outward behavior but ignored those commandments which can only be obeyed inwardly as the result of a surrendered will. Outwardly they looked "beautiful." Inwardly, they were full of covetousness and self-indulgence. On the outside, they appeared to be clean. Within, they had no concern for others. It was all a big show.

These same words could be expressed to many in our churches today: "Woe to you, pseudo-believers! You go to church every Sunday. You pay your tithes. You say grace before every meal and read a promise every day. But your lack of true godliness is shown by your lack of concern for others. You live for yourself and have next to nothing left over for others. Outwardly you appear righteous to men, but inwardly you are full of hypocrisy and lawlessness."

Jesus' words to the Pharisees were not a display of aggravation but a final attempt to *awaken and save them*. Nobody likes to hear hard words, but sometimes a strong rebuke is the only thing that will snap a person out of his delusion. Paul said to Timothy, "Preach the word; be ready in season and out of season; *reprove, rebuke*, exhort, with great patience and instruction. For the time will come when they will not endure sound doctrine." (2 Timothy 4:2-3)

Spiritual experiences alone do not provide evidence of conversion.[§] People can sense the presence or workings of God at some point in their lives or even feel His overwhelming love, but that does not necessarily mean they are saved! Jesus said, "Not everyone who says to Me, 'Lord, Lord,' will enter the kingdom of heaven; but he who does the will of My Father who is in heaven. Many will say to Me on that day, 'Lord, Lord, did we not prophesy in Your name, and in Your name cast out demons, and in Your name perform many miracles?' And then I will declare to them, 'I never knew you; depart from Me, you who practice lawlessness.'" (Matthew 7:21-23) Thus did Jesus indict many who seemed to be heavily involved in the work of God, even to the point of tapping into His power. How could they do miracles and still be sent to hell? I don't know. I only know that Jesus said it will happen. He gives the reason: they did not do "the will of My Father who is in heaven," but practiced lawlessness. Basically, *they did not obey God*, and they did not really live for God.

The dangerous thing about savoring God's love and presence while in self-will is that a person can walk away from such an experience in utter delusion. In the story of the rich young ruler, Mark tells us specifically that Jesus, looking at him, LOVED him. I am sure His love manifested itself as a

---

§   The apostle John gave two basic proofs of salvation: obedience to God's Word (1 John 2:3-5) and sacrificial love for others (1 John 3:14-19). By these "we know that we have passed out of death into life."

powerful emanation from His very heart—something the young man could feel. Nonetheless, his eternity depended upon *his response* to that ardent love. Would he obey the words of Jesus or not? Jesus in His mercy brought him to a crossroads, a point of decision. The man had to choose between Jesus and mammon. The issue is obedience, not feelings. The person who has truly been converted obeys God from the heart, becoming a vessel of God's love to others.

WHEN GRACE ABOUNDED

In the 1930s, the evangelical movement in Germany was very strong. Although there was gross idolatry and sin present, most of the German people of that day were simple folks—like their counterparts in the United States—whose lives revolved around church and family.

Dietrich Bonhoeffer, one of the Christian leaders of Germany in that era, could see the beginnings of a movement that greatly concerned him. Its foundational beliefs rested upon a faulty concept of grace: once a person is a Christian, no amount of sin can change his spiritual standing with God. Bonhoeffer desperately tried to oppose this ungodly movement before it could gain any further ground. Before losing his life at the hands of the Nazis, he penned these immortal words in his classic, *The Cost of Discipleship*.

Cheap grace is the deadly enemy of our Church. We are fighting today for costly grace.

Cheap grace means grace sold on the market like cheapjacks' wares. The sacraments, the forgiveness of sin, and the consolations of religion are thrown away at cut prices. Grace is represented as the Church's inexhaustible treasury, from which she showers blessings with generous hands, without asking questions or fixing limits. Grace without price; grace without cost! The essence of grace, we suppose, is that the account has been paid in advance; and, because it has been paid, everything can be had for nothing. Since the cost was infinite, the possibilities of using and spending it are infinite. What would grace be if it were not cheap?

Cheap grace is the preaching of forgiveness without requiring repentance, baptism without church discipline, Communion without confession, absolution without personal confession. Cheap grace is grace without discipleship, grace without the cross, grace without Jesus Christ, living and incarnate....

Costly grace is the treasure hidden in the field; for the sake of it a man will gladly go and sell all that he has. It is the pearl of great price to buy which the merchant will sell all his goods....

Such grace is *costly* because it calls us to follow, and it is *grace* because it calls us to follow *Jesus Christ*. It is costly because it costs a man his life, and it is grace because it gives a man the only true life.[4]

Unfortunately, by and large, the German people rejected his teachings. As the German economy prospered under the dynamic leadership of Adolph Hitler, spiritual life in Germany grew increasingly cold. The worries of the world, and the deceitfulness of riches, and the desires for other things entered in and choked the word, and it became unfruitful. (Mark 4:19) Life was getting better in the Reichland under the able leadership of the Fuhrer. National pride was restored. The "Christian nation" of Germany put Adolph Hitler into power because he gave them what they wanted. Not only did they install him as their chancellor, but *they adored him*! And before they knew what had happened, he was gassing Jews and other "undesirables" by the millions in the death camps of Europe. When they elected Hitler, they never dreamed he would perpetrate such atrocities! The absence of total surrender to Christ and the resulting lack of discernment made them vulnerable to the powerful personality of the Fuhrer.

We have so vilified the German people that it is easy to cast them all in the mold of Hitler. We forget that most of these were common people who, like us, just wanted to have a better life for themselves and their families. Once Hitler was in power, many of them became agents of butchery because their Christianity had no hold on their consciences and the moral climate of their day overpowered them. There was nothing to stop their descent into the cruelties of hell.

"We would *never* do what they did," we say. But dear reader, our culture is much more influenced by the spirit of Babylon than theirs was! We're in terrible danger of rolling out the welcome mat, not for a Nazi dictator, but for the man who will lead the world into a violent collision course with God Himself!

The people of America are ready for such a leader. The only real opposition that remains comes from the Christian Church. Unfortunately, much of this resistance is collapsing because of weak spiritual leadership. Poor discernment, selfish ambition and worldliness are all combining to leave the saints vulnerable to overwhelming deception.

"The churches are cluttered with religious amateurs culturally unfit to minister at the altar, and the people suffer as a consequence.... Much that is being done in Christ's name is false to Christ in that it is conceived by the flesh, incorporates fleshly methods, and seeks fleshly ends."[1]
-A.W. Tozer

"It is assumed that whoever is against [a certain] evil thereby represents Good. The possibility of his representing an even greater evil is [seldom] considered."[2]
-Lev Navrozov

8

Deception and Ambition at the Top

A worldly-minded church will embrace worldly concepts that inevitably pervert the Gospel of Jesus Christ and spawn false teachings. For example, concepts conceived in the New Age movement and in humanistic fields of "science" have already been quietly introduced into the Church, offering "another gospel" that accommodates selfish desires. The spirit of Babylon has woven its philosophy into the very fabric of modern Church theology and doctrine.

Where does the blame for this lay? Not at the grassroots level, but at the top, where leaders have been corrupted so often by deception and ambition.

As the apostle Paul made his farewell speech to the elders of the Ephesian church, he said the following:

> Be on guard for yourselves and for all the flock, among which the Holy Spirit has made you overseers, to shepherd the church of God which He purchased with His own blood. I know that after my departure *savage wolves* will come in

among you, not sparing the flock; and from among your own selves *men will arise, speaking perverse things*, to draw away the disciples after them. Therefore be on the alert, remembering that night and day for a period of three years I did not cease to admonish each one with tears. (Acts 20:28-31)

Just as Paul predicted, savage wolves did infiltrate the churches of the first century, and twenty centuries later we are seeing the same thing. Repeatedly, Jesus, Paul and the other apostolic writers warned of teachings that would lead people astray. Consider the following examples:

+ Paul also said that Satan disguises himself as an "angel of light," who carries out his evil intentions through false-hearted men. (2 Corinthians 11:14-15)
+ Jesus Himself alerted us that there would be "false prophets who come to you in sheep's clothing, but inwardly are ravenous wolves," (Matthew 7:15) and admonished us to judge "them by their fruits."
+ Peter cautioned us that "there will also be false teachers among you, who will secretly introduce destructive heresies... and many will follow their sensuality." (2 Peter 2:1-2)
+ John told us to "test the spirits to see whether they are from God... (or) the spirit of antichrist." (1 John 4:1-3)

These warnings are just as important for us today as they were to the first Christians. We must learn to be discerning about what people teach us. We must pray that God will give us ears to hear and eyes to see!

SINCERE BUT WRONG

When most Christians think of false teachers, the descriptions that Jesus and Paul gave come to their minds. But instead of looking for sheep, they look for wolves. Instead of looking for angels of light, they look for servants of Satan, such as obvious cult leaders. What many fail to realize is that false teachers *appear* as sheep and angels. When Jesus warned of false prophets coming in the last days, He was not primarily referring to cult leaders like Jim Jones or David Koresh. He said, "*Many* false prophets will arise, and will mislead *many*." (Matthew 24:11) He was describing deception that would occur on a much grander scale than that of a few isolated cult leaders. The wolves in sheep clothing and the angels of light are not *outside* the Church but *inside* it! They are not recognized as deceivers because their behavior is not what the Church expects to see in a deceiver.

There are two types of deceivers at work in the Body of Christ today. There are those who willfully lie to others to achieve their own selfish purposes. Television preachers begging for "seed faith offerings," men who prey on vulnerable women, and unregenerate entertainers who are tapping into the lucrative gospel music industry are all examples of wolves in sheep clothing.

Not so obvious—but just as devastating—are those who are not purposely leading the sheep astray. They spread false doctrine because that's what they have learned and they unwittingly pass it on to others. That is what makes the deception so powerful! The spirit of the world, which is now using them to dismiss the unvarnished words of Jesus in favor of a softer, more appealing message, has duped them. It is a watered-down gospel, with little or no fire in it. It is false because it is not the Gospel that was given by Jesus Christ.

Blind Ambition

While many pastors and ministers do their best to help people, others work intensely at creating personal followings. They want big ministry, with their names out front and with themselves as the CENTER. It is so easy for people's motives to get skewed in ministry. It is possible to begin a work for God with a genuine desire to help others, but the temptation to use it as a vehicle for personal success can be overwhelming. What begins as a sincere desire to do good often becomes a driving ambition to reach the top.

False teaching is one of the inevitable side effects of ambition within Christendom. When making it to the top becomes the primary motivation, desire for truth gradually becomes secondary.

Paul observed this very thing happening in the early church. He told the Philippians that some were proclaiming Christ "out of selfish ambition, rather than from pure motives." (Philippians 1:17) In the beginning of the next chapter of that same epistle, Paul said the following: "Do nothing from selfishness or empty conceit, but with humility of mind let each of you regard one another as more important than himself; do not merely look out for your own personal interests, but also for the interests of others." (Philippians 2:3-4)

These latter two verses are the heart of Christianity and are especially relevant to those in the ministry, whose calling is to serve others rather than themselves. Jesus faced this problem with His own disciples, who argued amongst themselves about who was the greatest. To their self-seeking attitude He responded, "If anyone wants to be first, he shall be last of all, and servant of all." (Mark 9:35) We have drifted away from this servant mindset. Instead of seeking to serve, many are seeking to put themselves in the "chief seats... and places of honor." (Mark 12:39) This is exactly what Paul predicted when he warned that false teachers would rise up "to draw away the disciples after them."

Intense competition to attract the largest crowds, the biggest audiences or the most readers leads to bubbly books and frothy sermons, lacking in both substance and conviction. Radio and television themselves create a pressure on the speaker to hold the listener's attention without offending him, simply because offended listeners don't send in the money needed to pay the astronomical expense of keeping the programs on the air. Confrontational preaching which assails sin, worldliness and carnality does not tend to draw a mass following.

To the typical watcher or listener, personality rates higher than content. He is star-struck, enamored with inflated personalities who appear larger-than-life. Media does that to its players, though it does not necessarily mean the principles are evil. However, end-time believers must listen carefully for error and reject it no matter who the messenger is.

WORLDLY-MINDED TEACHERS

Another cause of deception at the top traces to the substitution of education for anointing and to the desire behind that substitution: to gain credibility with the world. In the 1940s, '50s, and '60s, our leading Christian Bible colleges and seminaries, apparently in the hopes of gaining credibility (and accreditation) in the secular academic world, introduced the liberal arts into their curricula. Many of these classes, taught from a biblical perspective, were free of any polluting influence (i.e., mathematics, history, etc.) and were beneficial to the student's future in ministry. However, as we will discover in the next chapter, other liberal arts subjects eventually became a Trojan horse, transporting subtle deception into the Body of Christ. Bible colleges that had once been extremely godly institutions gradually lost their fire and wilted under the oppressive spirit of the world.

A lady who experienced this first-hand gives the following account as to what happened at her school.

In the early '60s, I attended a 3-year Pentecostal Bible school that emphasized preparing people for the ministry. Every student there planned on a life of service to God, whether it was pastoring a church or going on the mission field. The only classes offered at this school were either directly related to ministry or a study of the Bible.

The president of the school often preached to the students about the need to be sanctified. He taught us that any worthwhile ministry would only come as a result of a crucified life. In a day when *The Dick Van Dyke Show* was typical of what was on television, he continually warned us that TV watching would deplete our spiritual lives. His own deep consecration to God established a sober and serious atmosphere there.

During the course of my time there, we began hearing reports that denominational leaders wanted to bring liberal arts classes into the curriculum. The rumors going around were that the school was going to receive accreditation and begin offering 4-year bachelor's degrees. There were those students who were happy to hear this, but most wanted things to remain the way they were.

One day, the school president stood before us with tears streaming down his cheeks. He had been under tremendous pressure from the denominational headquarters to cooperate with their plans but had steadfastly resisted to the end. They finally forced him to resign. He gave us a talk that day that deeply affected my life. He warned us that there would be a lighter tone in the school in the future but not to allow ourselves to lose our sense of spiritual sobriety. Sometime after he left, we heard that he had died a brokenhearted man. Just as he predicted, the emphasis of the school underwent a great transformation. The deep sense of God's Spirit that had been there in earlier years was gone.

This dear lady's story is an illustration of what has occurred in a larger sense to almost the entire field of Christian education. Rather than discipling young people into godly living, they are being taught to become "professionals." Instead of emphasizing the importance of one's walk with God, subjects such as church growth are emphasized. The measure of one's godliness is not humility and inward purity but outward success. Today's worldly teachings will produce tomorrow's worldly leaders.

CONFIDENT ASSERTIONS

There is another factor at the teaching/preaching level in the Church that contributes to a marked decline in spiritual understanding and to the deception that follows: *spiritual immaturity covered up by confident assertions.* When it comes to discipleship, a teacher or preacher can bring others only as far as he's gone himself and no further. That becomes a real problem when the teacher wants to appear more spiritual than is actually true of him. Relying on his own charisma and personal abilities, he overreaches. He simply doesn't possess a true understanding of his subject. The result is shallow ministry and a superficial perspective.

The apostle Paul brought out this disparity when he wrote to Timothy:

> But the goal of our instruction is love from a pure heart and a good conscience and a sincere faith. For some men, straying from these things, have turned aside to fruitless discussion, wanting to be teachers of the Law, even though they do not understand either what they are saying or the matters about which they make confident assertions.
> (1 Timothy 1:5-7)

Paul spoke with authority because he had an intimate relationship with the Lord that was based on a life of deep consecration and prayer. Sincere love for others motivated him, not self-ambition.

The lack of these two factors—an intimate relationship with God and the motivation of love—inevitably lead to false doctrine or a watered-down message. Add in the human desire to have respect as a teacher without the willingness to earn it and the corruption spreads. It is all too easy to "lean on one's own understanding." Once a teacher learns to trust in his own abilities, rather than to live in meekness and humility, he adopts the attitude that always has worked in his past: *confidence and swagger*. As Paul said, "wanting to be teachers of the Law, even though they do not understand either what they are saying or the matters about which they make confident assertions."

Con(fidence) men have often taken advantage of simple, trusting folks. Is there any reason to believe it doesn't happen in the Church?

Years ago, before I entered ministry, I worked in a sales position for a while. I developed a friendly competition with one of the other salesmen, but no matter how hard I worked, putting in extra hours and making numerous calls, Rob always managed to out-sell me every month. The difference was Rob's winsome personality. In ten minutes, he could make a person feel like they had been friends for years. With a smile that never left his face, he could get people to sign on the dotted line just like that!

I see a lot of "Robs" in church leadership today. They are gifted with the ability to attract followers—not because they preach the truth, but because of their charming and winsome ways. In contrast, it is interesting to see what Paul said about himself in that respect:

> And when I came to you, brethren, I did not come with superiority of speech or of wisdom, proclaiming to you the testimony of God. For I determined to know nothing among you except Jesus Christ, and Him crucified. And I was with you in weakness and in fear and in much

trembling. And my message and my preaching were not in persuasive words of wisdom, but in demonstration of the Spirit and of power, that your faith should not rest on the wisdom of men, but on the power of God. (1 Corinthians 2:1-5)

It should come as no surprise then, that there were those in the church of Corinth who said of Paul, "His letters are weighty and strong, but his personal presence is unimpressive, and his speech contemptible." (2 Corinthians 10:10) Paul did not deny this. The question is: Would today's average church member be able to discern the Spirit of God in his words, or would they be bored by his uncharismatic preaching?

Big Business

Still another reason for deception and ambition at the top is the undeniable fact that *Christianity in the United States is a multi-billion-dollar industry.* Music CDs, books, teaching CDs and DVDs, seminars, conferences, and love offerings are all part of the bounty to be tapped into. This affluence encourages anybody with talent, abilities, and charisma to make it big. Unquestionably, success pays them handsomely.

Paul spoke of this when he said some were "peddling the word of God" (2 Corinthians 2:17) and "using godliness as a means of gain." (1 Timothy 6:5) How sad this is in light of the price our early Christian fathers paid for the sake of the Gospel! There are many in the ministry who are in it only for immediate and tangible rewards.

One example of the mentality that is prevalent in so much of the Church is the conversation I had with one of the country's leading Christian publishers. He had looked this book over and dismissed it as irrelevant. "Steve, what you need to do is write a book telling Christians how they can lose weight and be spiritual at the same time. Then you'll have a successful book!" The frightening thing is that this man meant what he said. One look at his publishing empire will tell the discerning soul that book sales are much more important than spiritual truth.

The deeper issue here is the Americanized mentality of business success transferred to the ministry. Where are the ministries whose watchword is SACRIFICE?

One experienced missionary tells the following story:

Recently I counseled a couple planning to enter missionary service. They claimed they desperately wanted to serve the Lord. They were well-qualified, and it was obvious that the Holy Spirit was calling them into the privilege of His service.

But the world had a grip on them. They began to ask what I now recognize as the critical American questions about Christian service. If they went into missions, how would they live? Would they have a home? Would they have a retirement plan? What about the education of their children? What about insurance?

They were measuring the opportunity for service by the amount of inconvenience it would cause them. They didn't want to face the possibility of difficulties, sorrows, sacrifice and uncertainty in missionary service. The risks were too great, and so, like millions of other North Americans, they have not yet obeyed that call. They probably never will.

What a contrast with the routine sacrifices made by so many Christian workers in the Third World. I think of a team of five young pioneer missionaries whom the Lord called to begin a mission in Rajasthan, a North Indian state. They had no money for train fare, let alone for food or rent. Everyone discouraged them and begged them to stay home. But this was their answer: "If we have no money to go by train, we will walk (1,500 miles). If one of us becomes sick and dies on the way, we will bury him on the roadside, and the rest of us will continue on. If only one of us survives the journey and reaches Rajasthan, and places only one gospel tract on the hot desert sand of that state before he dies, we will have filled our mission, and we will have obeyed our Lord."[3]

I am afraid that as long as ministers long for tangible material rewards, the American Church will continue to be deceived by leaders whose motivation is selfish ambition and carnal thinking and whose legacy is a weak gospel and false teachings. In the meantime, true men of God will find themselves ignored by lay people who prefer charisma to godliness and flash to spiritual substance. A Church that is open to worldliness will be open to deception.

"Right feeling is produced by
obedience, never vice versa."[1]
-Oswald Chambers

"Our only refuge, our only resource, our only strength,
our only comfort, our only authority, is the precious
Word of God. Take away that, and we have absolutely
nothing; give us that, and we want no more."[2]
-Charles H. Mackintosh

9

THE WISDOM OF KOSMOS

The following story epitomizes the state of the American Church as a whole: void of true spiritual discernment and quick to embrace the world's wisdom. The scene is another uneventful September afternoon in the life of Wes Allen.* As a department head in a large denominational headquarters, Wes was well respected and highly esteemed by all who knew him. Yet, unbeknownst to him, his reputation was coming under a demonic attack at that very hour.

Across town a Christian psychotherapist was counseling Amy, Wes's eighteen-year-old daughter. Probing to find the root of Amy's "deep-seated problems," the counselor gradually introduced the idea that Amy's father had molested her during childhood. At first, Amy recoiled at such a suggestion. But as the therapist skillfully pursued this line of thought, she began "remembering" incidents. Gradually Amy turned against her father, whose subsequent efforts to reason with her only strengthened her conviction that the psychotherapist was right.

* A pseudonym.

The therapist immediately brought her "findings" to Wes Allen's superiors, and subsequently, he was fired. Infuriated by these false charges, he sued the counselor and won the case after his daughter recanted of her "memories." In the end, having been exonerated of all charges against him, Wes's fractured relationship with his daughter was restored and he was reinstated to his former position with the denomination.

A worldly, problem-laden Church is susceptible to worldly solutions. In response to the great need that overwhelms our churches, the spirit of Babylon has commissioned an entire industry of professionals to dispense just enough help to keep people from experiencing a genuine breaking before God in true repentance. Rather than embrace the biblical concepts of self-denial and death to self, all too often believers run to "experts" who provide alternative answers that keep people locked in a prison of self-centeredness. The Church has enthusiastically embraced this worldly approach. We have reached the absurd conclusion that just because a Christian has a degree in psychology, he is qualified to teach people how to live a victorious life in Christ!

John MacArthur expounds on this:

> Scripture is the manual for all "soul work" and is so comprehensive in the diagnosis and treatment of every spiritual matter that, energized by the Holy Spirit in the believer, it leads to making one like Jesus Christ. This is the process of biblical sanctification....
>
> "Christian psychology" as the term is used today is an oxymoron. The word *psychology* no longer speaks of studying the soul; instead it describes a diverse menagerie of therapies and theories that are fundamentally humanistic. The presuppositions and most of the doctrine of psychology cannot be successfully integrated with Christian truth. Moreover, the infusion of psychology into

the teaching of the church has blurred the line between behavior modification and sanctification.

The path to wholeness is the path of spiritual sanctification.[3]

In 1 Corinthians, Paul describes what we would call "the Western Mind." He says, "The Greeks [Gentiles] seek after wisdom." (1 Corinthians 1:22) This proclivity to exalt human wisdom is a primary roadblock facing believers who want deep, true, victorious living in Christ Jesus. God doesn't expect us to be mindless robots, but He does command us to "set our minds on things above" and seek the mind of Christ in all things. Our problem stems from our tendency to approach spiritual matters with the natural thinking of the fallen mind, which is a perpetual antagonist of God. Paul said that "the mind set on the flesh is hostile toward God; for it does not subject itself to the law of God, for it is not even able to do so." (Romans 8:7) His point is that the natural processes of the human mind work completely differently than those of the Spirit.

Humans are inherently self-centered; our thinking constantly revolves around self. The pride and selfishness that result from this kind of thinking are in opposition to the way the Spirit of God thinks. Because a basic conflict exists between the two (Galatians 5:17), even the most brilliant person will unfortunately never enter the Kingdom of God unless he humbles himself as a little child. (Matthew 18:3-4) As believers, it is imperative that we come down out of our high-mindedness and learn that spiritual problems *cannot* be understood or deduced through human logic alone.

Let's be honest. For the most part, the Church in America is worldly, carnal and self-centered. It is bogged down with despondent, defeated Christians whose lives have spiraled wildly out of control in our permissive and prosperous culture. The inevitable result is that many struggle with an oppressing load of deep-seated emotional problems and addictions. The Church has lost sight of its cure for them and can now only offer a painkiller called "counseling" to dull the ache. There are very few in positions of influence anymore who understand what it means to come to Calvary. "Old-timers" with a strong testimony of walking in the Spirit have died off with no one to replace them. The teachings of *kosmos* have slithered under the door and slowly, methodically brainwashed us. *It is time to awaken out of our slumber and open our eyes to the deception that has overtaken us.*

The Wisdom of Kosmos - Entire Universe or whole Creation

To the Corinthian believers, who were forever searching out new philosophies and ideas, Paul said:

> Now we have received, not the spirit of the world (*kosmos*), but the Spirit who is from God, that we might know the things freely given to us by God, which things we also speak, not in words taught by human wisdom, but in those taught by the Spirit, combining spiritual thoughts with spiritual words. But a natural man does not accept the things of the Spirit of God; for they are foolishness to him, and he cannot understand them, because they are spiritually appraised. (1 Corinthians 2:12-14)

He went on to tell them that because of their immaturity, he was unable to speak to them as people with spiritual discernment, "but as to men of flesh, as to babes in Christ." (1 Corinthians 3:1)

The Corinthians were infatuated with the wisdom of this world. Over and over again, Paul reminded them that the wisdom of *kosmos* was foolishness to God. "We speak God's wisdom in a mystery," he said, "the wisdom which none of the rulers of this age has understood." (1 Corinthians 2:7-8) Worldly wisdom appeals to man's logical mind and to the self-life. Babylon demeans the way of the Cross and exalts self-preservation and the pursuit of personal happiness. Nowhere is this conflict of ideas more clearly laid out than in the words of Jesus: "If anyone wishes to come after Me, let him deny himself.... For whoever wishes to save his life shall lose it, but whoever loses his life for My sake, he is the one who will save it." (Luke 9:23-24) This way of thinking is diametrically opposite to the thinking *kosmos* promotes and puts a finger right on the reason Christians in America have so many unresolved problems: *an unwillingness to deny self.*

After thirty-plus years of working with people who have deep-seated problems, we at Pure Life Ministries have learned that only Jesus Christ has the power to bring a person into true joy and contentment—but He does have that power! Those who learn the secret of heart obedience and total surrender to His will come to know that blessed state of being.

Many want help from God, but they want it on their terms. They want the Lord to solve their problems without making any demands on their lives. "Zap me and fix me," is their prayer, but they are unwilling to live in submission, obedience and unselfishness. They want God to take away their troubles without their having to relinquish the pleasure-seeking lifestyle that produces the obsessive behavior in the first place. In short, they want the Lord to make them problem-free without disrupting the flow of their lives in this world. What they want is the victory of Calvary without the Cross of Calvary—an impossibility.

The Church has bought into the idea that if you have a medical problem, you go to a doctor; if you have a spiritual problem, you go to a minister; and if you have an emotional problem, you go to a psychologist. Thus, the *spirit of kosmos* was able to slip false teachings into the Body of Christ under the guise of professionalism.

At a time in my life when I was still deep in sin, I used to say to myself, "If only I had the money for a psychologist (or even better yet a psychiatrist), I could get the help I really need." The field of psychology always held a certain mystique for me. "Surely these probers of mind and behavior possess a knowledge that empowers them to liberate people like me," I reasoned. I studied psychology in school and immersed myself in trendy theories. I put my confidence in it because I believed it was a well-established science—this despite its failure to help me overcome my own problems. When I became a Christian, I transferred this trust to "Christian psychology" and its teachings. It was only after attending Bible school, where I was taught true biblical counseling, that I came to see how misplaced my trust had been.

The Modern Science of Psychology

One of the fallacies of psychology is that it is a fact-based science in the same sense that one would think of neurology or physiology. Nothing could be further from the truth, as Dave Hunt clearly shows:

> Early in December 1985, 7000 participants (3000 were turned away for lack of space) gathered in Phoenix, Arizona, for the "Evolution of Psychotherapy Conference." Billed by its organizers as "probably the largest gathering ever devoted to the practice of psychotherapy," the prestigious convention drew participants from 29 countries. One of the major features was the presence of psychology's remaining living masters, such as Carl Rogers, Rollo May, R.D. Laing, Joseph Wolpe, Albert Ellis, Bruno Bettelheim, and Thomas Szasz.
>
> The huge convention presented a strange dichotomy: On the one hand was the shocking display of confusion and contradiction; on the other hand, in apparent blindness

to the bankruptcy of their own profession, there was the enthusiastic and competitive planning by participants for the expansion of their influence upon a gullible public that eagerly looks to them for answers which they obviously don't have. *Los Angeles Times* staff writer Ann Japenga reported, "The heroes were there to evaluate where psychotherapy has come in 100 years and where it might be going—except they really could not agree on either."

The convention failed to settle differences among psychotherapy's hundreds of rival sects and bring some semblance of order to the chaotic muddle of literally thousands of conflicting theories and therapies.[4]

Agreement among psychologists is lacking because they reject the authoritative teaching of the Word of God in favor of human reasoning about the soul. Most of their theories are based on subjective analysis, not on empirical science. And even empirical science can't come up with any better explanation for abnormal behavior except to say, "It's in the genes."

The words of James apply to the confusion found in the realm of psychotherapy when he wrote the following:

> This wisdom is not that which comes down from above, but is earthly, natural, demonic. For where jealousy and selfish ambition exist, there is (confusion) and every evil thing. But the wisdom from above is first pure, then peaceable, gentle, reasonable, full of mercy and good fruits, unwavering, without hypocrisy. (James 3:15-17)

The truth is that the field of psychology is nothing more than a quagmire of confusing, conflicting theories about how to bring a person into emotional wellbeing. These pseudo-experts will never understand the true path into inner joy because they are unwilling to humble themselves before God.

Consequently, they grope around in the darkness of Babylon, in a vain attempt to come up with something—anything—that sounds like a plausible answer to man's problems.

Can we really expect that godless men like Sigmund Freud, Carl Jung or Carl Rogers—all of whom have been openly hostile toward Christianity—could provide solutions for the struggling Christian? If their solutions were what Christians needed (as contradictory as they are), why didn't God reveal them to godly men? Jesus Christ has been transforming people for two thousand years. Why is it that the Church suddenly feels she must crawl on her hands and knees to the unsaved world to find solutions for the problems of her sheep? The Bible claims that the Lord "has granted to us everything pertaining to life and godliness," (2 Peter 1:3) and that we are made "complete in Christ." (Colossians 2:10) What will it take for us to believe the Bible's own promises?!

A typical example of how we are told that we should put our faith in psychologists rather than God comes from the following quote in a *Christianity Today* article dealing with women addicted to pornography: "Women addicted to porn need professional therapy with a Christian counselor....The worst thing you can do with these women is lecture them about praying more or asking God for help. They've already done that, often to the point of despair."[5] Make no mistake about it: This is the voice of darkness cloaked in friendly words of advice from a professional. It appeals to human logic, common sense and past history, rather than encouraging faith in a mighty and a compassionate God who can and will set people free of their bondages (something I have witnessed on countless occasions during my 30-plus years of ministry). But it also offers a clear-cut choice for believers: Will you put your trust in worldly wisdom or will you obey and trust the Lord? "For the word of the cross is to those who are perishing foolishness, but to us who are being saved it is the power of God." (1 Corinthians 1:18)

The Best of Both Worlds—Or, The Conflict of Rival Religions?

The leading proponents of "Christian psychology" claim that they have been able to integrate the powerful truths of Scripture with those of psychology. Not adhering to the "simplistic teachings" of the Bible, nor to the lack of spiritual insight of secular psychology, they claim that they can provide their followers with the best of both worlds. Imagine that! At first glance, this reasoning seems to make sense, but when an honest person looks beneath the surface, he quickly comes to the realization that this is impossible.

The truth is that it is no more possible to combine the truths of Scripture with the fallacies of psychology than to integrate Christianity with Hinduism. Their underlying suppositions conflict and their differences are irreconcilable. What some call Christian counseling is really nothing more than the same old worn out teachings of psychotherapy masked by a thin veneer of Scripture. Verses are wrenched out of context to ostensibly give biblical support to their theories.

Dr. Jay Adams responds to this line of reasoning:

> You can be sure that it is not the result of common grace that two rival ways of counseling exist side by side! God cannot be charged with such contradiction. His common grace is not responsible for false teachings by Freud (man is not responsible for his sin), Rogers (man is essentially good and needs no outside help) or even Skinner (man is only an animal, without value, freedom or dignity). It is nearly blasphemous to claim (as a number do) that such systems, full of errors, falsehoods and Antichristian teachings, are the product of God's common grace! Imagine God, in common grace, through these systems, teaching people to believe that their problems can be solved apart from Christ!...

It is improper to conceive of Freud, Rogers and scores of others like them as great benefactors of the church, near Christians, or persons from whom we can learn much. No; rather, we must see clearly that they have come peddling wares of the enemy. They are his agents. They offer systems, counsel and a way of life opposed to biblical truth. Their views are not supplemental, but outright alternatives. Surely, they themselves see this clearly enough, and make no bones about it. They plainly say that there is no place for God or His Word. How is it, then, that some Christians are virtually blind to this fact?

In the final analysis, the answer to that question is this— Christians are duped into the acceptance of pagan thought and practice in counseling *when they do not think theologically*.[6]

Dave Hunt came up with much the same conclusion when he began investigating psychology in the Church:

In spite of their impotence to provide any lasting help, psychotherapies by the thousands have become almost as much a part of life as motherhood and apple pie. Consequently, the average Christian is not even aware that to consult a psychotherapist is much the same as turning oneself over to the priest of any rival religion. Of course, when it is practiced by a Christian, psychology is given an unwarranted legitimacy that deceives the unwary. Fallacy is still fallacy, and it is no less dangerous even when proclaimed or practiced by Christians.[7]

The basic assertion that interrelational conflicts, sinful habits, anxieties, fears, depression, and so on, can be resolved in the life of a believer from any source outside of Christ is false, misleading and unacceptable. Psychotherapy is the world's *alternative* to what God offers to the obedient Christian. The best that psychotherapy can hope to provide is merely a cheap imitation of the abundant life which is available to any true follower of Christ. By offering a counterfeit in place of God, Satan masterfully keeps people from running to the Lord in their need. They are "rescued" from coming to the place of desperation that leads to true brokenness, repentance and subsequent victory. Psychotherapy also undercuts the authority of Scripture. Today's believer is taught that his real hope is not to be found in the teachings of the Bible but in those of the world. This mentality is constantly reinforced on Christian radio, at the Christian bookstore, and often from the pulpit. The teachings of psychology are not a benefit to the Body of Christ but a definite detriment.

Perhaps part of the reason believers have so readily accepted the world's answers to their problems has been because they have become so infused with its mindset. There is no question that God created the human mind to be susceptible to outside influences—the very reason His Word is so powerful to mold one's thinking. It is the believer's responsibility to exercise extreme discernment and care over what he allows into his mind.

"Set a strong guard about thy outward senses; these are Satan's landing places, especially the eye and the ear."[1]

-William Gurnall

"If we were not so intoxicated with travel, pleasure, vacations, and recreation, would we not have more time to pray? If we were not so enamored of sports and entertainment, would we not have more time to pray? We have more leisure than ever before—but less time to pray. We are not only cheating God and the world but we are cheating ourselves."[2]

-Paul Billheimer

10

INDOCTRINATION

Ray was very excited when he came to see me one morning in 1996. One of a handful of men who continued to live at the Pure Life facility after completing the Residential Program, he held a special place in my heart. Ray was a young man grappling with the conflict between the messages and values of the Bible and those of 21st century American life. I appreciated Ray's walk with God, because, though he often made mistakes, eventually he would see his error and repent. He had a prevailing conviction deep in his heart that always seemed to straighten out his course when he would get off track.

"Pastor Steve, I saw the most awesome thing last night! I went over to a friend's house and watched the Tyson-Holyfield fight." Ray knew that it was against the ministry rules to watch network television, so I was a bit surprised at first by his boldness. Apparently, whatever he had to tell me was so marvelous that it would more than compensate for his infraction. "Holyfield knocked out Tyson, and after the fight he told the whole world that God had given him the strength to do it! He gave God all the glory for his victory! It was such a powerful testimony for the Lord!"

I did not say much to Ray, but his comments troubled me. His lack of discernment and willingness to break ministry rules were bad enough. Even more disturbing was the realization that Ray's lack of discernment reflected the loss of Christian perceptions and values across the moral board in the American Church of our day.

No one can deny that boxing is a brutal sport. Having been briefly involved with the sport in my younger days, I know something of what these men go through as professional fighters. Any career prizefighter suffers a considerable number of blows to the head. The cauliflower ears and smashed nose are only outward signs of the cumulative harm done to a boxer's head. The eventual loss of his mental capacity is the more frightening aspect of the physical damage boxing has inflicted on him.

The thought of the Spirit of Christ, the Lowly One, the meek Lamb of God, empowering someone to beat another man senseless in this way is absolutely absurd. (cf. Psalm 11:5) What is downright discouraging is that most American Christians would completely miss the contradiction in all of this.

AMERICANS FIRST

One of our primary problems as American Christians is that we allow the mores of our society to influence our lives more than God. To state it another way, our lives have been shaped more by popular American culture than by God's Word. Life for the newly-saved believer in the United States generally goes on much the same as it did prior to his confession of Christ as Lord of his life. Sadly, even after we are saved, we remain Americans first.

I do not think most believers in our country realize the extent to which American culture has molded their viewpoints and personal opinions. We have been systematically indoctrinated to pursue the "American Dream," while failing to recognize that the spirit of Babylon is driving our pursuit. The New Testament makes it abundantly clear that we must break with any cultural pattern that interferes with the life of sacrificial love Christ commands us to live. In the words of George Verwer, "We must not allow ourselves to be swept into the soul-binding curse of modern-day materialistic thinking and living."[3]

The message America broadcasts is "You, you, you. It's always about *you*" (an exact quote from a health insurance company's billboard). Why is it that we fail to discern how anti-Christ this message is? Is it because we have been taught to believe that it is the right way of thinking? From the time of infancy we have been openly encouraged to look out for number one, to be somebody, to get ahead, to fight for our rights, and so forth. It should be no surprise that when a person comes to Christ after years of listening to these affirmations of self-interest, he needs the Word of God to reshape his thinking and reorder his values. "Therefore if any man is in Christ, he is a new creature," Paul wrote. "The old things have passed away; behold, new things have come." (2 Corinthians 5:17)

Moreover, the genuineness of a person's conversion should dictate how seriously he examines these "old things" in light of the "new things." Part of the old things that should pass away are the daily indulgences that conflict with God's desires. Centering one's life on entertainment and selfish pleasure is the norm for the typical American, but what about for the believer? If life goes on much the same after conversion as it did before, is the person truly living in light of what the Bible teaches? Does he really desire to have the mind of Christ? Is he doing what Jesus would do? Should that person be convinced that he has experienced spiritual regeneration?

Christians should be citizens of heaven first and citizens of the U.S. second. Saints should be more concerned about the acceptable practices of their new life in Christ than those that made up their lives before Christ. Sure, they conform to the acceptable outward appearances of Christianity and quickly adopt the latest Christian lingo. But do they truly get to the place where they cease to be "conformed to the world?" Most followers of Christ seem to be torn between two lovers.

We need to look no further than our passion to be entertained to see the reality of this tug-of-war. America has become so addicted to entertainment that we cannot conceive of life without it. Americans play cards, board games, golf, baseball, soccer and football. They go swimming, biking, bowling, boating and fishing. They go to the movies, the beach, amusement parks, shopping malls and outlet centers. They read newspapers, magazines, romance novels and tabloids. They surf the internet, visit chat rooms, rent movies, play video games and spend endless hours sitting in front of a television screen. In short, there is no end to our indulgences when it comes to entertainment.

A.W. Tozer, one of the great Christian thinkers of the 20th century, made the following observation:

> There are millions who cannot live without amusement; life without some form of entertainment for them is simply intolerable; they look forward to the blessed relief afforded by professional entertainers and other forms of psychological narcotics as a dope addict looks to his daily shot of heroin. Without them they could not summon courage to face existence.[4]

While it is true that most of the activities mentioned above are harmless in and of themselves, the thing to consider is, "Where does all of this leave God in our lives?" The reality for most church-goers is that He has been crowded out of their lives.

Indoctrination

We have been trained to accept the American entertainment system as a normal part of life, yet the pleasure messages from Hollywood and Madison Avenue feverishly oppose the "preaching of the Cross." If we are going to make a clean break with the spirit of Babylon, then we will first need to break with the pleasures of worldly entertainment.

The Medium of Television

It is obvious to me that television has shaped our culture more than any other medium, person or event since it was mass-produced in 1948. It has been the great common denominator of life for the last fifty years, and there's little doubt it will continue to hold enormous influence over our lives in the 21st century. Life in America has become increasingly centered on watching television. It is one of those American household necessities that we take for granted. How many Christians even put forth the effort to ask God about its effect on their lives?

To our shame, Christian leaders have been largely silent on something that has done enormous harm to the Body of Christ. We must instead turn to secular media experts to learn of television's effect upon people's lives.

Carol Gentry, a writer for the *St. Petersburg Times*, cited researchers in an article she wrote entitled, "Slaves to the Set: U.S. Hooked on TV":

> In two days of presentations on the effects of television on the human mind, researchers concluded that television:
> + Is far more powerful than many people think and works in ways that are not yet understood.
> + Is at least habit-forming and possibly addictive.
> + Delivers an insidious message: that the ability to buy things is the highest goal in life.
> + Millions of Americans are so hooked on TV that

they fit the criteria for substance abuse in the official psychiatric manual, says Kubey, co-author of *Television and the Quality of Life: How Viewing Shapes Everyday Experience.*

+ Heavy viewers display five dependency symptoms, he says, two more than necessary to arrive at a clinical diagnosis of substance abuse.

+ While meaning to watch only a program or two, most TV viewers end up watching hour after hour. This is similar to the mistake made by alcoholics who think they can have just one drink, or former smokers who think one cigarette won't hurt.

+ Even those who recognize that they watch too much television don't seem able to cut down. "I can't tell you the number of people who've told me they had to get rid of the set or drop their cable subscription to control it," Kubey says. "They feel powerless."

+ Important family or personal activities get canceled or reduced to fit in with television. Health suffers, since heavy viewers don't get much exercise. So do family relationships....

+ Withdrawal symptoms set in when heavy viewers stop or cut back. During the period of readjustment, Kubey says, "some families will experience more conflict, stress and tension."

+ Those who watch a great deal of television get less enjoyment from it than those who watch less, the researcher found.

+ Yet the habit is a powerful one because a flick of the button produces instant relaxation much like the effect of a Valium. "Television is the cheapest, easiest and most readily available means ever invented for escape," Kubey says. "It shouldn't surprise us that people grow dependent on the medium."[5]

INDOCTRINATION

To put it bluntly, most American Christians are already TV (and/or internet) addicts. Is the spirit of the world behind this addictive quality? Is *kosmos* the drug? One thing is certain about television: it has permeated the entire population of this country with the spirit and message of Babylon.

Statistics indicate that the average American will see over 9,000 sexual situations on television per year, nearly all of which will be illicit encounters.[6] What kind of a message is that implanting in the hearts of believers? Christians will watch hundreds of hours of illicit sex, violent behavior, greed, crime and storylines depicting life without God. Born-again believers will immerse their minds in godless television plots under the guise of "needing a break." Can we really be so naive as to think a Christian's faith, conduct and testimony are uninjured in the process?

When a person spends hours each week viewing stories that involve ungodly behavior, his attitude toward sin in his own life will be greatly affected. If a man watches scenes of adultery and fornication night after night, how can he be convicted about the wickedness of lusting after some girl at work? His moral standards and beliefs most certainly will be eroded by what he has seen and heard. The more flagrant sin he views, the smaller his "little sins" will seem. Television desensitizes its viewers to the wrongness of sin and stifles the convicting voice of the Holy Spirit.

Drama has the power to manipulate the emotions and alter what people accept as fact. The viewer looks at life through the actors' lives. Scriptwriters inject their own ungodly beliefs into storylines. The sinful lifestyles of television characters consistently convey the message that sin is not only acceptable but even advantageous to the one committing it. Consequently, the images, situations, language and beliefs of the characters are projected into the viewers' minds, only to resurface powerfully later. This is especially true if a viewer forms an emotional attachment to the actors and actresses who portray such situations. It becomes increasingly easy to identify with the thoughts, decisions and lifestyles of the characters. The result? Sin is easily justified, rationalized, minimized and overlooked.

For any Christian to think that he can regularly watch television and not be adversely affected by its long-term, cumulative effects is pure foolishness. Television caters to every appetite of the flesh. It constantly presents the "lust of the flesh, the lust of the eye, and the boastful pride of life" in a positive light. Television distorts reality, tells lies and glorifies short-term solutions. Its actors and actresses personify the flesh, living out all its sordid fantasies. Do we really believe we are immune to such pernicious messages? Or do we love *kosmos* so much that we cannot bear to silence its voice in our homes?

SEARCHING FOR A COMPROMISE

I despair of finding any good, wholesome programs or movies on modern TV at all. We look for an element of compromise to be found in all of this. One can still find old reruns of *I Love Lucy* and *The Andy Griffith Show* that don't blatantly flaunt sin, but it seems that anything produced from the mid-sixties on carries one strong worldly theme or another in its storylines. Even Disney—once known for its innocent programming—now presents a definite New Age message in its movies.

However, even a benign show still keeps the believer in the enemy's arena. Whether it is in the suspense of an unfolding plot or in the excitement of a sporting event, Babylon is present, whispering its age-old mantra: *You can have a fulfilling life without God.* In the programs I mentioned, and thousands more, there is no turning to God, no seeking His will and no dependence on Him. The same title fits them all: *Life Without God.* Babylon drives people away from God and turns them in any direction other than toward Him. Success, money, power, relationships, pleasure and even possessions are the tricks of its trade.

Surely any honest and objective look at the effect this message has had on the Church will expose how much the daily lives of believers have been impacted. Let's face it; compromising Christians have allowed the spirit of the world to choke out a hunger for God's Word in their lives. (Mark 4:19) They have allowed television to play a more influential role in their lives than Scripture. The hedonistic message portrayed night after night on television has encouraged the pleasure-seeking lifestyle of the world rather than the self-denying message of Christ.

SPIRITUAL LETHARGY AND PASSIVITY

Another debilitating element of television is how it causes believers to be apathetic and spiritually passive. It literally saps people of the desire for the things of God. *Nothing will deaden a person's spiritual appetite like the spirit of Babylon.* The spirit of the world agitates the flesh and shuts out the Holy Spirit. The hunger deep within a believer's spirit for the satisfying presence of God is eclipsed by the soul's lust for entertainment. Not only does TV drain a person spiritually, but it also robs a person of precious time more profitably spent with family or in the pursuit of spiritual activities. With a beverage in his hand and junk food on his lap, the average TV watcher spends his time in a self-centered, imaginary world of escape. Have believers in the United States forgotten that we are in warfare? A.W. Tozer seemed to think so:

Men think of the world, not as a battleground but as a playground. We are not here to fight, we are here to frolic. We are not in a foreign land, we are at home. We are not getting ready to live, we are already living, and the best we can do is rid ourselves of our inhibitions and our frustrations and live this life to the full.[7]

Peter said, "Be sober, be vigilant; because your adversary the devil, walks about like a roaring lion, seeking whom he may devour." (1 Peter 5:8 NKJV) The words "sober" and "vigilant" stress the importance of mental alertness lest our minds become the devil's prey. We must be completely alert, like a sentry who anticipates an enemy attack at any moment. The enemy seizes his opportunity to attack when we are careless and lethargic. There's no excuse for passivity. Webster defines passive as, "Not active, but acted upon; affected by outside force or agency. Receiving or enduring without resistance or emotional reaction; submissive."[8]

By and large, American believers have become extremely passive. Rather than aggressively tearing down the strongholds of the enemy and waging a war for the souls of our loved ones, we have allowed the enemy to lull us to sleep and exploit us at will. Instead of affecting the world around us for the cause of Christ, we continue to permit this world's system to influence us. Consequently, we are unfit for war. We have become spiritually disarmed, fat and lazy. Paul said, "Suffer hardship with me, as a good soldier of Christ Jesus. No soldier in active service entangles himself in the affairs of everyday life, so that he may please the one who enlisted him as a soldier." (2 Timothy 2:3-4)

As followers of Christ, our primary calling is service, not self-satisfaction. We are to be soldiers, not gluttons. We are to be separated from the world, not slaves to its sensuality. In one poignant statement loaded with meaning for each of our lives, Paul wrote, "And do not be conformed to this world, but be transformed by the renewing of your mind, that you may prove what the will of God is, that which is good and acceptable and perfect." (Romans 12:2) Paul also says that God's will is transformation into the likeness of His Son. (Romans 8:29) How does this transformation occur? By the renewal of the mind.

How can our minds be renewed if we continually subject them to the godless programming of the world rather than to the soul-edifying message of Scripture? As Paul reminds believers, "You were taught, with regard to your former way of life, to put off your old self, which is being corrupted by its deceitful desires; to be made new in the attitude of your minds; and to put on the new self, created to be like God in true righteousness and holiness." (Ephesians 4:22-24 NIV) To the worldly-minded, all such urgent suggestions seem overboard and unnecessary.

A REFUGE FROM BABYLON

Ever since Adam and Eve's expulsion from the Garden of Eden, mankind has needed food, clothing, and shelter, i.e., a protective refuge from the elements. But in addition to those necessities, man also has a very real need for spiritual protection as well. Saints need a place where we can be free from the pollutions of Babylon. The spirit of the world beats against the heart- and mind-doors of every believer. This is virtually unavoidable and inevitable. When we go to work, the store, or out running errands, it is certain we will face devil-inspired messages in one form or another.

We are stained by Babylon in two ways. First, we are tempted to sin by sinners around us: a provoking coworker, immodestly dressed women, acquaintances who want to pull us into their sinful lifestyles and so on. Second, we are stained by the world through the media, whose message is communicated to us in a million subtle and even blatant ways. Billboards tell us about pleasures we need to experience. Department stores insist we keep up with current fashions. Magazine racks feature gossip about Hollywood stars. There's even a magazine called *SELF!* These are just a few examples of how we can be drawn into sinful thinking when we are in the devil's backyard.

This double-barreled assault upon us has a cumulative negative effect. Thank God, though we are IN the world, we don't have to be OF it! Our homes don't have to be filled with the message and spirit of Babylon.

I remember once going on a prayer walk down a deserted country road. At one point in the road there was a little bridge crossing over a creek. As I looked over the railing, there lay a water moccasin in the stream. It occurred to me that where I stood I was in no danger of that snake harming me, *unless I got down into the water with it.* This offers a poignant illustration for our spiritual lives as well: as long as we keep ourselves out of the old serpent's domain, there is little he can do to hurt us. Believers get bitten when they frolic in the enemy's territory.

As children of God, we need to do a thorough house cleaning, literally! We need to search out everything that the devil can use to keep us locked into the mindset of the world. Inspect closets, drawers, magazine racks, and music and video cabinets with an honest willingness to ask yourself if Jesus is displeased with anything in them. Every article that quenches the presence of the Holy Spirit in our homes must be removed if they are to become a sanctuary from Babylon. Make your home a place where every resident can calm himself after a day full of stress and rest with his family in true *koinonia* fellowship. Do as John Kilpatrick once suggested: pray over your home and declare it a NO SATAN ZONE!

Every believer is affected by the spirit of the world in one way or another. This is virtually unavoidable and inevitable. So then, what can we as Christians do? We cannot avoid being out in the world, but we can make choices that minimize its effects upon us. How? By taking care about where we go and by limiting the amount of time we spend in ungodly locations. We must also make absolutely sure that our homes are a spiritual refuge from the influences of the world's relentless pressure. If we can't make our homes a sanctuary from Babylon, what hope do we have of living separated, consecrated lives?

Many believers never know what it means to be spiritually clean. They are so immersed in the world that they cannot fathom life separated from it. I have spent the past three decades of my life living in a Christian community (Pure Life Ministries) in rural Kentucky. Having this separation for such a period of time has enabled me to better see how polluted I once was by this world's spirit and to discern more clearly the times in which we live.

SHAPING AND ESTABLISHING ACCEPTABLE NORMS

Have you ever wondered how national perspectives become established? How does "group think" come into being? Three examples come to mind, which point to how the enemy uses the media to shape and establish acceptable norms. First example: Why was it that when a young homosexual was beaten to death—a vicious crime to be sure—he was treated as if he were a martyr and a hero, but when a gang of angry homosexual militants attacked a group of Christians, it wasn't even mentioned? Who decided that one story should be emphasized while the other should be ignored? It was the liberal news media. Second example: Why is it that when the Beatles emerged in the early '60s that the youth in America immediately began emulating their looks and their lifestyle? Could it be because the media promoted them and made them appear larger than life? Third example: How did the national perspective on morality change so much in the past forty years? Isn't it because the media has continually pushed the limits of decency until now one can actually watch X-rated movies on cable television? You can be sure that the worldview of the writers, producers, actors and news people who control the media is diametrically opposed to the Lord's perspective. Why is that? Because the spirit of this world essentially controls most of the media and with it, our national mindset.

By and large, Christians are aware of the liberal bias in the news media, but I am not convinced that they are cognizant of how much their daily thinking is shaped by what they see, hear and read. They don't realize it because they are not spiritually discerning. And their lack of discernment is the result of insufficient soaking in the Word of God and over-soaking in the river of worldliness flowing into their minds via the media. The pressure to conform to the world's mentality is enormous. Paul said, "Don't let the world around you squeeze you into its own mold, but let God remold your minds from within." (Romans 12:2 PHP)

A Demonic Conspiracy

The spirit of *kosmos* is on a mission to control and utterly possess the minds of all people, including those who follow Christ. It seems clear to me that the invention of television is destined to play a much larger role in the fulfillment of end-time prophecy than most people think. To gain a perspective on this demonic conspiracy, I am including the following poem written in the early '60s, which gives clear insight into the strategy of the enemy.

THE DEVIL'S VISION
The devil once said to his demons below,
"Our work is progressing entirely too slow.
The holiness people stand in our way
Since they do not believe in the show or the play,
They teach that the carnival, circus and dance,
The tavern and honky-tonk with game of chance,
Drinking and smoking, these things are wrong;
That Christians don't mess with the ungodly throng;
They are quick to condemn everything we do
To cause believers to be not a few.

They claim that these things are all of the devil;
That Christian folks live on a much higher level.

INDOCTRINATION

Now, fellows, their theology, while perfectly true
Is blocking the work we are trying to do.
We will have to get busy and figure a plan
That will change their standards as fast as we can.
Now I have a vision of just what we can do,
Harken, I'll tell this deception to you;
Then find ye a wise, but degenerate man
Whom I can use to help work out this plan.

There's nothing so real as the things that you see;
The eyes and the mind and the heart will agree;
So what can be better than an object to view?
I say, it will work and convince not a few.
The home is the place for this sinful device,
The people deceived will think it quite nice.
The world will possess it, most Christians can't tell
That it is all of the devil and plotted in hell!
We'll sell them with pictures of the latest news
And while they're still looking, we'll advertise booze.

At first it will shock them; they'll seem in a daze,
But soon they'll be hardened and continue to gaze.
We'll give them some gospel that isn't too strong
And a few sacred songs to string them along.
They'll take in the ads, with the latest of fashions
And soon watch the shows that will stir evil passions.
Murder and lovemaking scenes they'll behold
Until their souls will be utterly cold.
The old family altar which once held such charm
Will soon lose its place without much alarm.
Praying in secret will also be lost
As they look at the screen without counting the cost.
The compromise preachers, who don't take their stand,
Will embrace this new vision and think it is grand.

They'll help fool the people and cause them to sin
By seeking this evil and taking it in.
Influence is great and this you can see;
Just look at my fall and you'll have to agree.
It won't take too long, my demons, to tell
That the vision of Satan will populate hell!

Divorce will increase, sex crimes will abound;
Much innocent blood will be spilled on the ground.
The home will be damned in short order I say,
When this vision of mine comes in to stay.
Get busy, my cohorts, and put this thing out;
We'll see if the church can continue to shout.
The holiness people who stand in our way
Will soon hush their crying against show and play.
We'll cover the earth with this devil vision
Then we'll camouflage it with the name television.

The people will think they are getting a treat
Till the Antichrist comes and takes over his seat.
He'll rule the world while the viewers behold
The face of the beast, to whom they were sold.
We'll win through deception, this cannot fail;
Though some holiness preachers against it will rail."[9]

CHAPTER POSTSCRIPT

Multitudes of professing Christians around the world
are sound asleep, in a drug-induced stupor. They have been
deceived by years of careful indoctrination via television
and other media. Occasionally someone disturbs their
slumber by ringing an alarm bell, but as a whole the Church
has remained lethargic. It is all too easy to dismiss one's
misgivings as unimportant. The sweet and soothing song
of Babylon always allays their fears. "Now, now," Satan

whispers, "there is nothing to be alarmed about. Go back to sleep. Everything is all right."

Without realizing it, many who claim Christ as Lord and Savior are slowly being prepared to hear another voice, which will not sound much different than the one they have heard for years. One day a man will appear on television with a tone and message they recognize easily: the familiar voice of Babylon.

But this time he will speak with an unprecedented force of deception that will be irresistible to those who have been prepared for it. The intensity of his deceptive power is incomprehensible to our minds. The arrogant attitude of Christians will be their undoing. The hypnotic power of the voice of Babylon PERSONIFIED will be more than they can resist. For many, it will be TOO LATE.

As Scripture foretells, this man, the Antichrist, will be "the one whose coming is in accord with the activity of Satan, with all power and signs and false wonders, and with all the deception of wickedness for those who perish, because they did not receive the love of the truth so as to be saved. And for this reason God will send upon them a deluding influence so that they might believe what is false, in order that they all may be judged who did not believe the truth, but took pleasure in wickedness." (2 Thessalonians 2:9-12)

The desire to be entertained is one of the lusts of the flesh the enemy uses to coax believers into his mindset, but there is another one that is even greater: covetousness. John used the phrase "lust of the eyes" to describe this passion which is so inherent in the fallen nature. The desire to accumulate the things this world offers is a powerful force, and we'll focus on this topic in the next chapter. First, however, I encourage you to pause and consider what the Lord has been saying to your heart.

"It is not poverty, but discontent
that makes a man unhappy."[1]
-Matthew Henry

"Temporal prosperity is too small a matter
to be worth fretting about; let the dogs have
their bones, and the swine their draft."[2]
-C.H. Spurgeon

"There is no happiness in having or in getting,
but only in giving. Half the world is on the
wrong scent in pursuit of happiness."[3]
-Henry Drummond

11

LIVING LIKE KINGS
(IN SATAN'S KINGDOM)

Citizens of the United States enjoy a level of prosperity that has never been experienced by any nation in the history of the world. Even today's lower middle class family lives with more luxuries than most kings of past centuries. What monarch of previous history ever enjoyed a flush toilet, a microwave oven, a television set (with instantaneous news from around the world), an automobile or a refrigerator? Unquestionably, the combination of great prosperity and technological progress has allowed the American people to live at a staggering level of opulence. This wasn't the result of happenstance. How did we arrive at such a place?

THE BIRTH OF CONSUMERISM

The Renaissance and the Reformation were not the only factors that helped to usher the world out of the dismal Dark Ages. One of the great movements of this new period in history began when the Puritans broke away from the Church of England and set sail for the coasts of the New World.

Their survival during that first cruel winter—due in part to the compassion of local Indians—was the motivation that lay behind their celebration of that first Thanksgiving Day. The Puritan work ethic—which not only saw work as noble but also as an act of devotion to God—became the foundation for progress in this nation. Hard work, and the success that followed, was their assurance that God was with them.

According to Rodney Clapp, author of "Why the Devil Takes VISA," as late as 1850, sixty percent of the nation worked on farms.[4] This rural population constructed their own homes and barns, fashioned their own tools, did their own sewing, made their own furniture, grew their own crops, and raised their own animals. On a whole, life for early Americans was devoid of the complexities and chaos that makes up modern society.

The Industrial Revolution, which began in the mid-19th century, brought enormous changes to the American culture. Factories sprung up in the larger cities, producing implements more cheaply and a great deal faster than any individual could do it. A great migration began as thousands left their farms to live in the cities and work in the factories. During the last half of the 19th Century, the value of manufactured goods in the United States rose a staggering 700 percent.[5]

Aided by the new efficiencies of manufacturing and mass production, factories began producing more goods than the country was currently consuming. Rather than cut back on production and diminish profits, manufacturers took a new tack, namely, salesmanship and advertising. They were so driven by the desire to gain more that eventually they led this country out of the wilderness of frugal living into the promised land of liberal spending. The practice of buying on credit lured people out of their cautious lifestyles; the temptation to "have it now" was overwhelming. Prior to this, people would literally save pennies to buy some item they desired, no matter how long it took to save up the pennies. Buying on credit meant they could have it immediately and pay it off in installments.

Manufacturers quickly realized the explosive potential in advertising and launched elaborate marketing schemes *en masse*. The days of bland classified ads for merchandise in the back of the newspaper soon became obsolete. Up to this point, people only looked in the advertisement pages when they needed a particular item. Now they could find slick advertisements on every page. This was the real turning point in American consumerism. For the first time, *people were purchasing merchandise they didn't need* and were not actively looking to buy. Advertisers had tapped into a powerful human passion: coveting lust.

In truly brilliant fashion, marketing experts learned how to create a certain *atmosphere* in order to sell their products. They quickly figured out that a good salesman does not focus on the item being sold but on its imagined benefits. For instance, the marketing people for Packard automobiles might have created a billboard with the picture of a family driving down some scenic highway in their new car. The effect this picture would have on the subconscious was that having a Packard gave a family freedom, excitement and luxury. Consequently, a couple might stop by a Packard dealer, "just to look around." Then, a well-trained salesman would go to work on them, furthering the illusion and at the same time creating just enough pressure to make it more desirable to buy the car than to leave without it. Since those early days, this same basic marketing tactic has been worked on people in countless ways and with millions of different products.

During the first half of the 20th century, manufacturers made steady, albeit slow, progress in the plan to transform the American citizen from a need-based to a desire-driven consumer. It was not until the post World War II era that this scheme exploded into full bloom as millions of Americans went into a buying frenzy. The United States soon became a credit-based nation as people ran up billions of dollars worth of debt over the next several decades.

Not satisfied with inducements for Americans to buy what they wanted, greedy retailers took the further step of purposely creating goods either to wear out quickly or to become out-of-date ("planned obsolescence"). In 1955, retailer Victor Lebow gave a glimpse into their marketing strategies when he stated, "Our enormously productive economy... demands that we make consumption our way of life, that we convert the buying and use of goods into rituals, that we seek our spiritual satisfaction, our ego satisfaction, in consumption.... We need things consumed, burned up, worn out, replaced, and discarded at an ever-increasing rate."[6]

Other than during brief economic recessions, consumer spending has increased exponentially. It is like a cute stray puppy taken in by an unsuspecting couple that turns out to be a St. Bernard and eats them out of house and home! Our little extravagances of the fifties and sixties have grown into a monster we can hardly feed. The massive U.S. debt is only an outward symptom of what has become a national disease. One day we'll have to pay the piper!

It is common knowledge that in the 19th century, one of the schemes employed by some companies was to increase profit margins by setting up "the company store." The owners would go into an area and build a shantytown for the workers, complete with a company-owned general store. Much of the laborer's paycheck would find its way back to the owners via the store. When money was short, the store would offer easy credit. If the debt grew beyond the worker's ability to repay it, he would find himself in the position of not being able to quit his job. He would, in essence, become little more than a slave worker for the company. Naturally this practice was very advantageous to the company owners, who actually encouraged it by offering easy credit.

The spirit of Babylon is doing this very same thing to Americans today. Every year, people find themselves going ever deeper into debt with the one who "comes only to steal, and kill, and destroy." (John 10:10) They are as locked into the slavery of covetousness as those workers were to the company store. The enslaving agent in their lives is not debt itself, but rather their love for the things of this world. Easy credit just puts those things within their grasp.

American living is characterized by an endless, selfish pursuit for more things and fresh experiences. The American Dream is simply "more for me and mine." We are constantly bombarded by the allurement of things we want. *The New York Times* estimated that U.S. citizens are typically confronted by some 3,500 advertisements per day.[7]

One would hope to find that such advertising has no affect on Christians, yet in this area believers differ very little from the unsaved. We work just as hard at "getting ahead." We are in just as much debt. We buy just as many unnecessary luxuries, deceived into believing this is symbolic of divine blessing. In short, if we are honest with ourselves, we have to admit we are every bit as driven in our desires as those outside of the evangelical community. Such covetousness makes a mockery of the Cross.

The Power of Coveting Lust

The sinfulness of coveting is greatly emphasized in the Bible. It is prohibited in the Ten Commandments. (Exodus 20:17) Jesus describes it as one of the evil passions of a man's heart. (Mark 7:22) Paul lists it as one of the characteristics of someone on his way to hell. (Ephesians 5:5)

There are two Greek words translated as "covet": *epithumeo*, which is usually translated as "lust" or "desire," and *pleonektes*, *covet—lust to or desire*

which means, "to be eager for more of something." The sin of coveting is the act of fixing one's desires upon some object and staying in a lust for it until it is possessed. It is one thing to want something; it is another matter altogether when a person covets it. The following analogy helps to illustrate the difference in these terms. Two Christian men enter the clothing section of a department store and notice a sharp looking suit on display. Neither man can afford it at the time. Each man's reaction to the suit reveals his spiritual condition. The one would like to have it but, realizing he cannot afford it, quickly dismisses the thought of purchasing it. The other covets it and is so compelled to have it that he buys it with his credit card, caving in to what John refers to as "the lust of the eyes."

Dave Harvey describes the difference between coveting lust and materialism:

> Materialism is fundamentally a focus on and a trust in what we can touch and possess. It describes the unchecked desire for, dependence on, and stockpiling of *stuff*. In some people it's more painfully obvious than in others. But it pervades every heart…
>
> Simply stated, coveting is *desiring stuff too much* or *desiring too much stuff*. It's replacing our delight in God with joy in stuff. Materialism is what happens when coveting has cash to spend. (Emphasis in original.)[8]

Coveting lust is the most underrated source of wickedness in American life. It is the sin most frequently omitted from the vocabulary of the American Church. Preachers are reluctant to bring it up. If it is mentioned in a message, it is usually touched on in a general, non-offensive way.

Regardless of this aversion in our churches, the Bible has much to say about it. Paul described this sin to his disciple Timothy. "But those who want to get rich fall into temptation and a snare and many foolish and harmful desires which plunge men into ruin and destruction. For the love of money is a root of all sorts of evil, and some by longing for it have wandered away from the faith, and pierced themselves with many a pang." (1 Timothy 6:9-10)

The desire to get ahead is one of the strongest passions in the heart of man. Covetousness, which lies behind this drive, is so powerful that Paul equates it to idolatry because it is in essence the worship of possessions. (Colossians 3:5; Ephesians 5:5) *Ouch!* The problem is not so much a love for the actual money itself but for the objects of desire it acquires. Christians are driven by this appetite without their giving it a second thought. Nevertheless, it would be wise for every child of God to examine their hearts. The devotion to money is extremely dangerous because it causes people to wander away from the faith. How many American Christians have completely wandered away from their life with God and yet are clueless about their desperate condition?

THE SOWER AND THE SEED

In the parable of the Sower and the Seed, Jesus described four types of soil, each of which represents a different state of heart. The third kind of soil is thorny with covetousness. Jesus said, "And others are the ones on whom seed was sown among the thorns; these are the ones who have heard the word, and the worries of the world, and the deceitfulness of riches, and the desires for other things enter in and choke the word, and it becomes unfruitful." (Mark 4:18-19) These "thorns" work hand in hand with each other. They represent the three steps a covetous person takes as he backslides from the simple truths of the Word of God.

Jesus is giving us a picture of someone who has just come to the Lord. Most people who have been born again experienced that blessed first love when thoughts of Jesus completely filled the mind. He meant everything to the person. The heart was full of joy. The outlook on life was fresh. The grass was greener. Everything was wonderful. Yet, Jesus said that along the way, "the desires for other things enter[ed] in and choke[d] the word." The heart, which had been so completely satisfied with Christ, has now allowed something very evil to slip back in. It is covetousness: wanting the things of the world. As the person continues to feed this beast, its appetite grows. The thorns of other attractions begin to overrun the person's heart. Before long, they completely take over, smothering and choking out the Word, which had once been so alive. Although the person has remained faithful in his church attendance, he has *wandered away from the faith* in his heart.

The Worries of Life

Several years ago, I spoke to a men's group about the need to simplify one's life. Afterwards a clean-cut, ambitious-looking young man came up to me to defend his lifestyle with the rationalization I have heard so many times before: "I just want to provide a good home for my family." I sensed he was determined to believe what he wanted to believe, so I nodded politely and did not respond. If the Lord had led me to, I would have asked him some pointed questions, such as:

+ You say your concern is for your family's well being. If that is truly what motivates your over-work/over-spend lifestyle, then why is it that you allow your family to watch hours of network television every night without concern about how it is affecting them?
+ Why is it that you do not have any time to spend with your young boy?
+ Why don't you take the time to intercede for your rebellious teenage daughter?
+ Why is there no family altar in your home?
+ Isn't it true, sir, that you are a workaholic, driven by

ambition to get ahead and by a passion to accumulate more possessions?

+ Are you sure it is their interests that concern you and not your own?

Of course, the sharpness of these words probably would have upset this man, which I did not want to do, but these are legitimate questions we should all consider. It's far too easy to underestimate the powerful pull of the charms of this world.

Once a person has begun to slip away from the Lord, he becomes entangled in "the worries of life," which are simply the responsibilities of life such as food, housing, clothing, transportation, schooling for the kids, insurance, bills and so forth. Responsible Christians do provide for their families, of course: Scripture even demands it. (1 Timothy 5:8) But Jesus commanded us not to allow the worry about such things to consume us. This was such an important issue that He devoted a large portion of the Sermon on the Mount to the subject. "Do not be anxious for your life!" He said. (Matthew 6:25) This was a commandment that equals "Do not commit adultery" in importance and yet it is treated as if it were a trifling suggestion by a patronizing grandfather. In all honesty, doesn't anxiety about money arise from fear, insecurity and lack of trust? Or even from an underlying aversion to discomfort? Instead of learning to "freely give" and to "seek first the kingdom of God" as Jesus taught, isn't it true that we focus too much of our attention on protecting our possessions in this world?

Jesus directly confronted this mindset when He said, "For whoever wishes to save his life shall lose it, but whoever loses his life for My sake, he is the one who will save it." (Luke 9:24) It is sinful to attempt to save the life we have been commanded to give away.

DECEIVED

If a person continues to give in to such covetousness, a creeping deception begins to permeate his heart. "The deceitfulness of riches" applies not only to the wealthy, but also to anyone who adopts the mindset of Babylon. The more one has, the more one wants. As Solomon once observed, "He who loves money will not be satisfied with money, nor he who loves abundance with its income." (Ecclesiastes 5:10) Money holds out the hope of prestige, possessions and pleasure—but riches lie! The materialistic person, driven by money's promise of fulfillment, will accumulate one thing after another, until one day, to his horror, he will discover that his soul is desolate. The seeker after success will someday reap the emptiness that comes with striving. The pleasure-seeker likewise will learn that he can't find the satisfaction he craves. Satan knows just how to tantalize people with the world's charms so they always keep reaching for more. IT IS ALL A GREAT DECEPTION.

In 1957, (taking inflation into account) the average American worker made less than half of what he made in the eighties. Did this make him happier? Not according to David Myers, author of *Society in the Balance*: "Since 1957, the number telling the University of Chicago's national Opinion Research Center that they are 'very happy' has declined from 35 to 29 percent. In fact, between 1956 and 1988, the percentage of Americans saying they were 'pretty well satisfied with your present financial situation' dropped from 42 to 30 percent."[9] One could only imagine how much worse off Americans have become since the eighties.

The drive for money and things only make people emptier and more spiritually depleted. John Wesley, discussing the deceitfulness of riches, said the following:

Deceitful indeed! for they smile, and betray; kiss, and smite into hell. They put out the eyes, harden the heart, steal away all the life of God; fill the soul with pride, anger, love of the world; make men enemies to the whole cross of Christ! And all the while are eagerly desired, and vehemently pursued, even by those who believe there is a God![10]

The greatest lie of prosperity is its ability to make people believe they are walking with the Lord when in reality they have long since drifted away from Him in their hearts. Like the Laodiceans in Revelations 3, they imagine their spiritual lives are going very well. But Jesus sees things much differently. The greed of materialism has eaten away their spiritual substance. To Jesus they look like children whose stomachs are bloated, not because they are full, but because they are dying of starvation! In the end, they will discover that they have "pierced themselves with many griefs," as Paul said to Timothy.

THE DESIRE FOR OTHER THINGS

Like any addiction, the lust for material gain has become a habit which must be maintained at any cost. Our maddening lust has silenced any concern one might have. We have been deceived by the tremendous power hidden within the great realm of DESIRE. Many, if not most believers, have sold themselves into the system of the Antichrist, which will one day demand allegiance as the cost of maintaining their lifestyle ("no one should be able to buy or to sell, except the one who has the mark, either the name of the beast or the number of his name." (Revelation 13:17)) Churchgoers who think they can live for years as slaves to Babylon and then suddenly declare their freedom from it are in a great delusion. Such people are preparing themselves to receive the mark of the beast. In a certain way, in their hearts they have already taken it.

When Satan offered the kingdoms and glory of this world to Jesus in return for His worship, *he showed the true longing of his heart.* The devil passionately craves the exaltation that belongs to God alone. Be careful if you are thinking, "Of course Jesus would turn him down. Why would He worship Satan?" It seems so simple to us to reject such a temptation. But do you realize the devil has put the same offer on the table to you? And many are accepting it without a second thought. They compromise a little here and a little there, but to their minds "it's no big deal." The subtlety of the offer obscures the enormity of what is happening. The devil is literally in the details. In the fine print is the one thing he really is after: *our very allegiance to his system.* The devil is not concerned about people "naming the name of Christ," as long as they are in fact still servants to his system. Hypocrisy is the devil's delight.

Paul, knowing full well how intoxicating this spirit can be, warned Timothy: "But flee from these things, you man of God; and pursue righteousness, godliness, faith, love, perseverance and gentleness." (1 Timothy 6:11) There is urgency in Paul's words that remind us of the angels' warning to Lot, "Escape for your life! Do not look behind you... lest you be swept away." (Genesis 19:17)

THE WAY OUT

Despite the tremendously deceptive power of materialism that is affecting the many, you can be among the few who turn things around. The man who has "entangle[d] himself in the affairs of everyday life," (2 Timothy 2:4) can disengage himself! Those who have become burdened by "the things of the world" can "lay aside every weight." (Hebrews 12:1 NKJV) The person who has become "conformed to this world," can "be transformed by the renewing of [his] mind." (Romans 12:2) It will require commitment, discipline and a new perspective on life in Christ Jesus, but it is well worth the effort to extricate oneself from the violent, overwhelming tug of Babylon.

If you are convicted about covetousness; if you know in your heart that Jesus deplores your wasteful spending habits;

if you sincerely want to change but are unsure how to go about it; to you I offer the following suggestions:

First, just *repent*. A real change of heart always begins with repentance. Examine your heart thoroughly. Get alone with God and study what the Bible says about greed, covetousness and money; also study what it says about giving. Allow the Lord to expose and root out every aspect of covetousness He reveals to you. Offer Him an itemized repentance list. Once you have done that, you are spiritually clean. The remaining steps will help you develop a new lifestyle.

Second, change your perspective about God. It is important that you begin seeing Him as your Provider and Blesser. Instead of treating yourself all the time, allow the Lord to have that place in your life. You may be surprised at how generous He really is! I can personally testify that the Lord has blessed me in ways I could never have done for myself. "Wait patiently for Him." You don't need everything you want, and you don't need it NOW.

Third, if you have debts, develop a plan to pay them off. Begin with the smallest balance and put every dime you can spare toward those bills. Sacrifice some of your indulgences. The inconvenience is nothing compared to how free you will feel when the debts are paid. Keep one credit card for emergencies if you must, but otherwise learn to live without them.

Finally, simplify your lifestyle. Admit you've been living extravagantly. Don't forget that what we call "the necessities of life" all come with a high price tag. It's amazing to discover how little you really need!

People are used to the obsessive merry-go-round of overwork and over-buy. The thought of choosing a different lifestyle has never occurred to them. But we have options. We don't have to live like kings in Satan's kingdom. We don't have to sell our souls to him. We can choose to simplify our lives. We can live at a more manageable level.

As you change your lifestyle, I also want to encourage you to follow the commandment of Jesus: "Do not lay up for yourselves treasures upon earth... but lay up for yourselves treasures in heaven." (Matthew 6:19-20)

D. L. Moody wrote the following pertinent words:

"Lay not up for yourselves treasures on earth." It looks a little stern, perhaps, but it must be right. After all, all that a man is really worth is what he has got in heaven. We bring nothing into this world, and it is certain we shall carry nothing out. Therefore God says, *Lay not*. The Christian who does, suffers. There is no gain in it. It is done at a terrible expense, the heart's desire in exchange for the soul's leanness. Here are two ships coming up a river. The first, full sail, cuts bravely through the water; the second creeps along, towed by another. She appears to be on the point of sinking, but still she floats. Why? Because she has a cargo of timber, and has become waterlogged. Lot was all right while he kept with his uncle Abraham, but when he left him, and got down into Sodom, he got a good deal of this world's goods, and grew waterlogged. So it is with many Christians. They have got waterlogged. They have got so much money that they cannot get into the harbor themselves, and they require others to help them in. The religious life gets sluggish. The spiritual pulse begins to beat slowly. "Why is it?" they say, "that we do not have more spiritual power, and more joy in the Lord?" The secret is easily found out. People who ask these questions have got their treasure here.

When men go up in balloons they take with them bags of sand for ballast, and when they want to rise higher they throw out some of the sand. Now there are some Christians who, before they rise higher, will have to throw out some ballast. It may be money, or any other worldly consideration, but if they wish to rise, they must get rid of it. If you have got overloaded, just throw out a little money, and you will mount up as on eagle's wings. Any minister will tell you what to do with it. I never saw any department of the Lord's work that did not want some money.[11]

✗ Jesus commands believers to lay up treasures in heaven. Every kind deed, every prayer offered for others, every moment of true worship, every act of selflessness are all being translated into spiritual currency and stored in a heavenly account with your name on it. We can deposit as much as we wish into our eternal savings account. That "money" is reserved for eternity and covered by God's infallible deposit insurance. If you were moving to a foreign country next year, wouldn't you think it wise to send money to a bank in that country before you left? Wouldn't it be a blessing to arrive there with a sizable balance in your foreign account?

We can expend our entire lives selfishly trying to live like kings and build up riches in Satan's kingdom, but as far as I am concerned, it's better to be an heir to the One who is putting Satan under His feet! We are headed into the final moments of the history of mankind. It is time to prepare ourselves for what lies ahead!

PART THREE

THE CHURCH IN THE LAST DAYS

"Where, oh where is the trumpet voice of the church warning men to flee from the wrath to come? Surely there are millions of believers who say that they believe Jesus may come today, yet they live in carnality. They talk more about the rapture than about this picture of our mighty Savior, the Christ of God."

-Leonard Ravenhill

"The Bible looks on sin, not as a disease, but as
red-handed rebellion against the domination of the
Creator. The essence of sin is—'I won't allow anybody
to "boss" me saving myself', and it may manifest itself
in a morally good man as well as in a morally bad
man. Sin has not to do with morality or immorality,
it has to do with my claim to my right to myself,
a deliberate and emphatic independence of God,
though I veneer it over with Christian phraseology."[1]
-Oswald Chambers

"Because man is born a rebel, he is unaware he is one."[2]
-A.W. Tozer

12

The Spirit
of Antichrist

There seems to be an escalating interest in the Christian community regarding the end times and who will be the Antichrist. Will one of the leaders of the European Union suddenly assume worldwide power? Will a New Age guru promise to bring an end to all of man's problems and emerge as a world leader? Whoever it may be, we know that one day he will direct an all-out insurrection against God.

Variously referred to as "the beast," "the lawless one," "the little horn," and so on, this "Man of Sin" will be so imbued with the anti-Christ spirit of the devil that he will become *the* Antichrist. Nevertheless, believers need not be overly concerned with this man's identity. It will not be a mere man who drives the world into a collision course with God that will one day end at Armageddon. Rather, it is *the spirit that will possess the man* who will orchestrate the events leading up to this final great conflict. The man himself will be nothing more than a devil-possessed psychopath who serves as Satan's pawn.

Intoxicated with Babylon

It is absolutely vital that believers realize they are under a withering spiritual assault from this rebel spirit right at this very moment. The power of the spirit of Babylon is like a heavy cloud resting upon this earth, continually promoting anti-Christian messages and luring people to remain (or become) independent of God's authority. It is this atmosphere which is paving the way for the great insurrection at Armageddon.

The Spirit of this Age

Most people would agree that the decade of the '60s marked a major turning point for the United States. In 1960, the biggest concerns of most young people were finishing school and preparing for the future. They were proud to be Americans and looked forward to getting a piece of the prosperity pie for themselves. People still lived with a general sense of respect for authority. Employers were often authoritative and employees accepted it as part of life. Generally speaking, people simply did what they were told.

However, within a short time all of this changed. Suddenly, the morality of our nation took a major nose-dive as public prayer was banned in the nation's schools, social and political unrest became more pronounced, and the debacle called the Vietnam War got underway. By the end of the decade, drug abuse was rampant, sexual promiscuity was the norm, and anti-government riots were taking place across the land. What happened to "America the Beautiful?"

It seems evident that during the early '60s a demonic force was quietly unleashed upon the earth. As that evil assault gained in strength, wickedness increased proportionately. (Daniel 7, 11; 2 Thessalonians 2) We have become so desensitized to reports about terrorist acts, genocide, school shootings and brutal murders, that we hardly realize the degree of darkness that has surrounded us.

As time goes on, we can expect things to get worse. Not only will evil escalate, but also the number of people giving over to it will multiply. The Bible accurately describes this period of world history as a time when young people are "disobedient to parents" (2 Timothy 3:2) and "lawlessness is increased." (Matthew 24:12)

The decade of the '60s ushered in a radical mentality that has worked its way deeply into our hearts and minds. When older Americans were hit with the first wave of this new thinking, it was dismissed as "just a phase that young people go through." However, by the beginning of the 1990s, the young people of the 1960s were in control of the country, and American culture began to reflect the ideology and social mores of this wayward generation. Bumper stickers such as *Question Authority*, *If It Feels Good Do It*, and *No Fear* expressed the new attitude. Even some segments of the older population adopted it. The rising power of the spirit of Antichrist began uniting us in a national disdain for righteous authority.

THE MYSTERY OF LAWLESSNESS

Though the Law of God in the nation of Israel often was disobeyed and disregarded in its long history, it still played a major role in the daily life of a Jew. The Law (Hebrew, *torah*) governed his relationship to God as well as his relationship with other Jews. As a sacred written code, it formed the basis for rule and conduct and served as a very powerful bonding agent for the Jewish people.

However, the concept of law (Greek, *nomos*) goes beyond the commandments of God given in the Pentateuch. In fact, every culture, no matter how primitive (or how rebellious to God's prescribed law), has a set of customs which establish what is to be considered right and wrong for that particular society. The primary meaning of *nomos* is "what is proper," and the opposite of *nomos* is *anomos*, which means to live without law or to adopt an attitude of lawlessness. According to Vine's

Expository Dictionary, *anomos* means more than committing an unlawful act; it means "flagrant defiance of the known will of God."[3] Anyone who lives in self-will is *anomos*—lawless.

Babylon the Great is a "mystery" according to Revelation 13:5, perhaps because of the dark, cryptic rituals of the Babylonian religion. Shrouded in its infamous history are secrets modern man may never uncover. More importantly, however, is Babylon's prominence as *the designation for everything which has opposed God throughout all history.* But there is another mystery as well. Paul said, "For the mystery of *lawlessness* is already at work; only he who now restrains will do so until he is taken out of the way. And then that lawless one will be revealed." (2 Thessalonians 2:7-8a) This worldwide rebellion against God is what David predicted a thousand years before when he wrote the second Psalm:

> Why are the nations in an uproar, and the peoples devising a vain thing? The kings of the earth take their stand, and the rulers take counsel together against the LORD and against His Anointed: "Let us tear their fetters apart, and cast away their cords from us!" ...
>
> Now therefore, O kings, show discernment; take warning, O judges of the earth. Worship the LORD with reverence, and rejoice with trembling. Do homage to the Son, lest He become angry, and you perish in the way, for His wrath may soon be kindled. How blessed are all who take refuge in Him! (Psalm 2:1-3, 10-12)

Establishing the state of all-out anarchy spoken of here is precisely what the enemy must forge among "the nations," "the peoples," "the kings of the earth," and "the rulers" before "the lawless one" can be revealed. Then, with lawlessness being the global hallmark, the way will be paved for the Antichrist who will seek to bring his version of "peace" and set up his authority in the world.

LAWLESSNESS IN THE CHURCH

This attitude of rebellion has spilled over into the lives of believers. Had Babylon blatantly tried to thrust its mentality on the Church, the attempt would have failed. Our leaders would have set aside their differences and become unified in their opposition to it. However, Satan is much too crafty for such a frontal assault. Rather, he has beguiled the Church by a subtle, slow and *mysterious* attack on our standards of godliness. What the spirit of Antichrist could never have done overtly, it has accomplished by stealth.

Little by little, one corruption after another has been introduced into the framework and corporate mentality of American Christianity to the point where the Church has lost its moorings. The changes in the last forty years have lowered standards for today's ministers below the standards of yesterday's layperson! Anyone whose conscience urges him to abstain from worldliness is mocked and labeled a fanatic. And the definition of "worldliness" is so watered down that the worldliness I'm talking about involves activities which would have shocked believers of a generation ago!

The daily saturation of alarming news and illicit behavior via television, newspapers, magazines, and the internet has left Christians spiritually and emotionally numb. It's hard to be affected by anything. Images of the wicked behavior of lawless people fill our minds, stain our souls and influence our hearts. We've become so corrupted that we no longer even feel the need for holiness! It is understandable for the world to think a zealous believer is strange, but for the Church to view a consecrated saint with suspicion, derision and even contempt shows how corporately backslidden Christendom truly is.

Unfortunately, the media is not the only purveyor of lawlessness to the Church. As we saw in chapter nine, the teachings of psychology have crept into the Christian arena quietly and unnoticed. By overemphasizing what they call "dysfunctional" upbringing, psychotherapists have turned us all into "victims." Consequently, we have lost the sense of personal responsibility for our actions, even though the Bible requires it. Psychological rationalization for sinful behavior stifles the Holy Spirit's ability to convict people of their sin and allows the "victim" to rattle off excuses for what he's done. "I drink because I was raised in the home of an alcoholic." "I get mad at others because my father was mean." "I regularly indulge in sexual fantasy because God created me with these needs and does not expect me to resist my natural urges." Whatever happened to old fashioned conviction for sin? Where is the heartfelt cry for God's purity? Where is the hunger and thirst for righteousness? Why aren't we hearing strong preaching about the need to walk in the Spirit? Where is the fear of the Lord in the Body of Christ?

In His last-days discourse, Jesus said, "Because lawlessness is increased, most people's love will grow cold." (Matthew 24:12) The meaning of "the mystery of lawlessness" goes beyond the idea of isolated acts of disobedience to God. It refers to an independent mindset; an attitude that one can pick and choose when he will obey the Lord. To a large extent Christians are allowing themselves to join forces with the lawless spirit that grips the world.

THE REFUSAL TO REPENT

We are now entering the time when lawlessness will reach the greatest heights ever known in the history of mankind. Evil is more intense than ever before. The forces of darkness are enjoying their greatest power. Sexual perversion is now at epidemic proportions around the world. The sign that evil has reached its peak—the final stage of lawlessness—is *a stubborn refusal to repent*. Three times we are told in the Book of Revelation that people "would not repent of their deeds." (Revelation 9:20-21; 16:9, 11)

Do you recall the opening words of the ministry of both John the Baptist and Jesus? "Repent, for the kingdom of heaven is at hand." (Matthew 3:3 and 4:17) The Kingdom was at hand because the KING was at hand! Truly the proper response to the King's presence is humble obeisance. He is the KING; we are His subjects, prostrate before Him. The right steps are confession of sin, repentance, and faith in His mercy. Every activity contrary to His will instantly comes to an end.

If that was the way to prepare for the first coming of Christ, it only stands to reason that it is also the way to prepare for His Second Coming. If Jesus is coming soon, then the need for repentance is greater than it has ever been. Unfortunately, people dislike repentance. They resent the exposing of their sinful thoughts and deeds. I have seen congregations listen to a godly evangelist preach his heart out, only to leave the meeting just as cold-hearted and unmoved as they were when they arrived. On the whole, those who profess Christianity have lost their sense of the evil nature of sin. The fear of God has been abandoned in favor of a superficial concept of His grace. People no longer feel obligated to change, to grow or even to please the Lord. In fact, many of those who claim to be His followers don't know what real repentance is. They've never done it!

THE GENUINE CONVERSION

In our day of civil liberties, it is difficult for us to comprehend what it was like for people living in biblical times under the authority of a king. He was a dictator with absolute control over every person in his kingdom. The fairness of this wasn't examined on CNN. The legality of it wasn't challenged in court by the ACLU. There were no protest marches outside the palace. The king's authority was simply accepted by his subjects as a part of life. Nobody would think of questioning it.

Occasionally, one king would decide to invade the kingdom of another. He knew if he won the ensuing battle, that everybody in that king's realm would become his subjects, including the other king himself. One Old Testament king boasted, "Seventy kings with their thumbs and their big toes cut off used to gather up scraps under my table." (Judges 1:7) When Nebuchadnezzar captured Jerusalem the second time, he had King Zedekiah's sons put to death in front of him, had his eyes gouged out, and sent him off as a broken man to Babylon in chains. When Ben-Hadad, the powerful king of Syria, decided he was going to attack the northern kingdom of Israel, he sent the following message to King Ahab: "Your silver and gold are mine, and the best of your wives and children are mine." The king of Israel answered, "Just as you say, my lord the king. I and all I have are yours." (1 Kings 20:3-4 NIV) When one king surrendered to another, he understood what it meant: "I and all I have are yours." It would be an unconditional surrender.

This is what the Christian conversion should resemble. The person's kingdom has been overthrown by a new King. He doesn't come out to face the new Master with a list of conditions! He's in trouble and he knows it. The enormity of his sin overwhelms him. The magnitude of his crimes against God staggers him. The reality of his unworthy condition is too great to bear. The knowledge of his utterly lost condition terrifies him. He has nothing to offer God. He realizes there isn't a thing he can do to save himself. It is in this condition that he comes to the King and says, "I and all I have are yours!" There, lying utterly prostrate before God, he is hoping for one thing and one thing only: MERCY.

Most people do not come to the Lord like that. They are not overwhelmed by the realization of their sinful condition. They are willing to change their lives to a reasonable extent if it means being saved from hell. They are willing to "switch sides" and align themselves with mainstream Christianity. They will learn who the popular radio personalities are, which books are considered "must reading," and what upscale church to attend. They adeptly adapt! They learn how to mimic those around them in words and deeds. Any sincere soul can only weep at the thought of how many lost people sit in evangelical churches.

As the enemy's activity increases in the days ahead, it is imperative that believers learn to live in a state of perpetual repentance. They must open their hearts to the searching of the Holy Spirit. They must continually turn away from carnality, worldliness and the pet sins that "so easily beset us." And most of all, they must repent of rebellion, lawlessness and self-will!

Scripture makes it clear that there will be a tremendous rise in falsehood at the end of the Age. Frankly, I am very concerned about the Church's readiness to face this onslaught. I don't believe we realize the magnitude of what is coming our way. In fact, I feel that most people who claim to be followers of Christ are in danger of being swept away by the greatest flood of deception that has ever been witnessed by mankind.

"The kingdom of Babylon is the original spin zone. It gains many of its followers through seduction and deception. Conversely, the beautiful aspect of the Kingdom of God is that it rules by truth rather than by half-truths and misrepresentations."[1]
-Steve Harrison

"Many have lost the favourable presence of God and are not aware of it. They have provoked God to withdraw from them but are not sensible of their loss nor ever complain of it. Their souls languish and grow weak. Their gifts wither. Everything goes cross with them and yet they impute not this to the right cause. They are not aware that God has departed from them nor are they in any care to reconcile themselves to him or to recover his favour."[2]
-Matthew Henry

13

THE GREAT DECEPTION

The present-day Church is very comparable to the Jewish people who were following Jesus during the height of His popularity. Everywhere He went multitudes hung on His every word and watched His every move. When He miraculously turned two fish and five barley loaves into a feast for five thousand, His awestruck followers exclaimed, "This is of a truth the Prophet who is to come into the world." (John 6:14) They were so enthralled by Jesus they were ready to make him king of Israel by force. He was not moved by popular emotion, however, and He certainly cared nothing for His reputation among the insincere. It was the pleasure of His Father that He sought and therefore He withdrew from the crowds and headed up the mountain for another night of prayer. (John 6:15)

The next day, the crowds found Him again. Their excitement remained at a fever pitch. They were ready to face the invincible might of Rome itself on His behalf! But things were not going to happen the way they imagined. The first words Jesus spoke to them established the course for what would follow: "Truly,

truly, I say to you, you seek Me, not because you saw signs, but because you ate of the loaves, and were filled. Do not work for the food which perishes, but for the food which endures to eternal life." (John 6:26-27)

These people were not seeking Him because they wanted the life in God that the signs pointed to but because they wanted Him to use His supernatural skills to enhance their lives on this earth. Their full bellies represented the earthly prosperity and power they were seeking. They were not as interested in serving God as they were in God serving them.

Not long after this He would say, "For life is more than food, and the body than clothing.... Do not seek what you shall eat... for all these things the nations of the world eagerly seek... but seek for His kingdom." (Luke 12:23, 29-31) Paul would later say, "The kingdom of God is not eating and drinking, but righteousness and peace and joy in the Holy Spirit." (Romans 14:17) He would also use the same analogy describing carnal ministers: "Whose end is destruction, whose God is their belly, and whose glory is in their shame, who mind earthly things." (Philippians 3:19)

It is interesting that end-time believers are warned about the same battle between carnal and spiritual appetites: "And just as it happened in the days of Noah, so it shall be also in the days of the Son of Man: they were eating, they were drinking, they were marrying, they were being given in marriage.... It was the same as happened in the days of Lot: they were eating, they were drinking, they were buying, they were selling, they were planting, they were building." (Luke 17:26-28)

Jesus knew it was the life in *kosmos* the people craved. In no way was He going to cater to their carnal desires and worldly thinking. As He began to speak truth, they became offended and angry. "I am the bread of life; he who comes to Me shall not hunger, and he who believes in Me shall never thirst." (John 6:35) What was their response to such a declaration? "The Jews therefore were grumbling about Him... saying, 'Is not this Jesus, the son of Joseph, whose father and mother we know? How does He now say, 'I have come down out of heaven'?" (John 6:41-42)

Blind, hardhearted, and lacking spiritual discernment, this disgruntled crowd was trying to understand the things of God with natural, earthbound thinking. Jesus' words were weighty and pertained to heavenly matters. He added to their confusion by saying, "He who eats My flesh and drinks My blood has eternal life, and I will raise him up on the last day." (John 6:54)

This was too much! His claims seemed weird to them. "This is a difficult statement; who can listen to it?" they asked incredulously. John, the faithful witness, records what happened next:

> As a result of this many of His disciples withdrew, and were not walking with Him anymore. Jesus said therefore to the twelve, "You do not want to go away also, do you?" Simon Peter answered Him, "Lord, to whom shall we go? You have words of eternal life. And we have believed and have come to know that You are the Holy One of God." (John 6:66-69)

As long as Jesus gave the people what they wanted, they were happy to be numbered among His disciples. They would have gladly lived out the rest of their lives following Him. But unlike many "user-friendly" pastors today, Jesus wasn't interested in multitudes for the sake of numbers. He wanted lifetime followers who were committed to live for the Kingdom of God, regardless of the cost. In His customary way He brought them to a crossroads. A decision would have to be made. Were they willing to follow Him in spite of the cost or would they turn away?

Today, just as in His day, many are happy to call themselves followers of Christ. Things are going fairly well for believers in America. Our bellies are full, our barns are overflowing and our possessions are increasing. In other words, everything is basically going our way, but whether we are brought to a definite fork in the road or not, God knows the true condition of our hearts.

THE CROSS ROAD

Christianity has always been a matter of the heart. God has a right to see if your religious activities spring from a deep inward consecration. (Amos 5:18-24) True Christianity begins and ends in the heart. Weak faith reveals weak commitment. Jesus said that many "receive the Word with joy," but fall away when their faith is tested. (Luke 8:13) Do you realize that *the falling away always begins in the heart?* The outward aspects of faith may continue, like going to church, tithing and so on, but somewhere along the line the inward state of our heart is going to be tested.

There is only one road to heaven, and it goes straight through the narrow gate of Calvary. Jesus said, "If anyone wishes to come after Me, let him deny himself, and take up his cross daily, and follow Me. For whoever wishes to save his life shall lose it, but whoever loses his life for My sake, he is the one who will save it. For what is a man profited if he gains the whole world, and loses or forfeits himself?" (Luke 9:23-25)

On another occasion, Jesus slightly altered the second statement: "He who loves his life (Greek, *psyche*) loses it; and he who hates his life (*psyche*) in this world (*kosmos*) shall keep it to life (*zoe*) eternal." (John 12:25) The deliberate choice of words for "life" sheds light on the real meaning. *Psyche* represents one's existence on earth, while *zoe* represents one's life in God. So Jesus was saying that whoever loves *his earthly existence* loses it; and he who hates *his existence in kosmos* shall keep it to *a life in God* forevermore.

That statement tests the purity of one's Christian commitment. Culture has a way of corrupting one's Christianity. A person's outward activities may be "Christian" while his inward allegiance is still in Babylon. In our culture, "the preaching of the cross is foolishness." (1 Corinthians 1:18) To the "many" who shun the narrow way, (Matthew 7:13) the Cross demands too much. It makes no logical sense to them because they approach Christianity from the mindset of Babylon. Beguiled by the low level of consecration they see around them, they protest inwardly, "Aren't the sacrifices I've made enough? I've given up drinking, cussing and fornicating. I 'deny myself' every Sunday morning by going to church when I feel like sleeping in." *But they have never been to Calvary inwardly where their old life has been crucified and a new life has begun.* Real surrender occurs when we choose the narrow way of the Cross. That's when the deep changes begin.

On the other hand, the few who have gone to Calvary (Matthew 7:14) see life eternal at the end of the narrow road. It changes the way they view this life. The temporal yields to the eternal. The inconsequential is replaced by the supremely important. This inward change has enabled saints down through the centuries to face hardship, opposition, persecution and even death. They lived out their Christian testimony in the environs of *kosmos*, but saw themselves as pilgrims in it, not citizens of it. We too must hate our lives in this world, as Jesus said we must. The book of Revelation reveals the fact that those who "overcome" the spirit of Antichrist "loved not their lives unto the death." (Revelation 12:11 KJV)

OVERWHELMING FALSEHOOD

In a vague sort of way most people believe we are now living in the last days. The signs of the times are certainly evident: the tremendous increase of knowledge, the great strides of technology, the movement toward a cashless society, the almost universal acceptance of perversion, the trend toward a one-world government and the adulteration of spiritual values all point to it. "Yes," we say glibly, "these surely are the last days!" And yet, life goes on as usual. The pressures of work, packed schedules and the hectic pace of life force spiritual considerations into the background. The concept of a one-world government in the hands of a devil-possessed leader makes for good reading but is not considered a relevant factor in their daily lives. "That may happen sometime in the future, but right now I'm just trying to keep my head above water," is the prevailing attitude. The thought of somehow being deceived by the devil into worshiping such a leader seems ridiculous to most.

Nevertheless, it is clear that Jesus and other New Testament writers saw it as a time of unprecedented deception. When asked about the sign of His return, the first thing Jesus said was, "Take care that you are not *deceived*. For many will come in My name claiming they are the Anointed One, and many poor souls will be *taken in*." (Matthew 24:4-5 Voice) The italicized words here are the translation of the Greek word *planao* which means, "to cause to wander astray into error, to seduce or deceive another." The fact that Jesus used this term three more times in His discourse about the last days shows the importance He placed on being spiritually alert to this vast deception. Nor was He the only one to utilize this term regarding the end of the age.

After discussing the great moral decline of the end times, Paul said, "In fact, evil men and false teachers will become worse and worse, *deceiving* many, they themselves having been *deceived* by Satan." (2 Timothy 3:13) Peter also had much to say about the dreadful days that lay before you and me. He especially zeroed in on the false teachers of our time, saying, "Abandoning the straight road, they went astray…" (2 Peter 2:15a) And in John's tremendous vision, he foresaw the culmination of deception at the end of the age when the spirit of Antichrist "*deceives* the inhabitants of the earth…" (Revelation 13:14a PHP)

These are clear warnings primarily spoken to those of us alive in the last days who are facing this unprecedented deception. If there is no reason to be concerned, I ask you, why all the strong warnings about it?

The Great Deception

A Bride in Trouble

The devil has already deceived the Christian Church in many ways, paving the way for even greater deception directly ahead. This assault is not something far off into the future: it is on our doorstep. The deception which is upon us is overwhelming and will only grow in intensity and pervasiveness.

The Church is in trouble for a number of reasons. First, she has lost her sense of the evil nature of sin. She no longer grieves over sin, carnality, and worldliness. Second, she has become addicted to the carnal lifestyle of Babylon, trading a love of the Father for the things of this world. Third, she is asleep and doesn't know it, mesmerized by the soothing voice of Babylon. Fourth, she has rebelled against God's authority.

When Paul described the coming world leader, he used the strongest possible terms:

> [He is] the one whose coming is in accord with the activity of Satan, with all power and signs and false wonders, and with all the deception of wickedness for those who perish, because they did not receive the love of the truth so as to be saved. And for this reason God will send upon them a deluding influence so that they might believe what is false, in order that they all may be judged who did not believe the truth, but took pleasure in wickedness. (2 Thessalonians 2:9-12)

This glimpse into the workings of the enemy during the end of the age requires a special examination. The Antichrist will make a great display of demonic power when he breaks upon the world scene, but to limit that display to obvious, outward demonic manifestations would be terribly shortsighted and mistaken. The two little phrases, "with all power and signs and false wonders," and "with all the deception of wickedness," indicate a deception of monstrous intensity and staggering magnitude—the likes of which the world has never seen before. We cannot even imagine the enormity of the evil force unleashed against mankind when the Man of Sin emerges because the deception becomes so utterly believable and plausible!

It is easy to make confident claims about how we will stand by Christ no matter what, but when demonic powers fill the atmosphere with their terrifying presence, even the best intentions will wither up and drain away. It is sheer nonsense for us to claim we can withstand the power of the enemy in our own strength. Man is no match for Satan's power. It is only by abiding in Christ that we have authority over the devil.*

CAUSE FOR CONCERN

Although the floodwaters of deception are rising and most believers are already standing on the slippery ground of compromise, a spiritual tsunami is rushing toward us that will shake everything that can be shaken. (Hebrews 12:25-29) The prospect of this unprecedented wave of evil would not be so alarming if the Church were mentally and spiritually prepared for it, but the very opposite is true. In fact, there are three prevailing attitudes that prove her unpreparedness.

First is the attitude, *I cannot be deceived.* We naturally believe that while others may be deceived, it will never happen to us. This is the very attitude the enemy counts on because it lulls people into a false sense of security. Someone once said, "If you think you can't be deceived, you're already half way there." This is precisely where the devil has many Christians today: halfway there.

The second attitude is *natural self-confidence.* "I don't care what happens or how bad it gets. I will never, ever, deny Christ."

---

* I believe in the security of the believer, but that security is found in Christ. I fear for those who presumptuously think they are abiding in Christ simply because they declare it while in reality they are still living for self and immersed in kosmos.

As we know from the experience of the disciples in the Garden of Gethsemane, self-confidence withers in the heat of spiritual warfare. Those who have a history of denying Christ in favor of the things of this world in their daily life will find they have no strength when the enemy comes in like a flood. If they routinely forsake the Lord inwardly now, how will they find the courage to stand for Him when they become confronted by the terrifying presence of Satan? This is sheer fantasy. As Jeremiah asked, "If you have run with footmen and they have tired you out, then how can you compete with horses? If you fall down in a land of peace, how will you do in the thicket of the Jordan?" (Jeremiah 12:5)

The third cause for concern is *the perverse tendency to prefer a lie to the truth*. Most Christians think that the most important aspect of truth is having correct doctrine. We can have correct doctrine without *abiding in the truth*. Biblical truth has a lot more to do with the integrity of our relationship with Jesus than it does with mental consent to orthodox theology.

I remember a time when two of my staff members attended a large gathering of men for a weekend of meetings. The preaching came off as shallow, as the speakers attempted to whip up fervor in the men through the use of emotional hype. The final speaker was the late Dr. Edwin Louis Cole. He delivered a refreshing message, direct and uncompromising. With humility and love he told the huge audience the truth about their spiritual condition and what they needed to do about it. Later, one of my staff members overheard someone complaining about that sermon, saying it was the only "negative message" of all the speakers. The Word brought that day seemed negative to this man *because he did not want the truth*. He preferred non-confrontive, emotion-driven preaching that told him what he wanted to hear. My staff members came away from the event disappointed in the overall attitude of the attendees. They lamented, "It's as if people are now saying, 'We don't want the truth! Tell us what makes us feel good!'"

What Paul predicted is happening right before our eyes: "For the time will come when they will not endure sound doctrine; but wanting to have their ears tickled, they will accumulate for themselves teachers in accordance to their own desires; and will turn away their ears from the truth, and will turn aside to myths." (2 Timothy 4:3-4)

One of the greatest needs of the corporate Body of Christ today is a love for the truth. The truth is there to receive for those who want it, but there is no denying that at times the truth does hurt. The flesh protects itself because we do not wish to face the implications that come with it. It is easier to ignore the truth or ridicule the messenger who speaks it. My dear friend, you will either be one who "receives the love of the truth so as to be saved," or you will "perish." You will either love the "preaching of the cross," or it will seem like "foolishness" to you.

The love of this world is in the heart of every person. The only way it is purged is through deep repentance and the process of sanctification described in chapter five. It must be exposed and expelled. Paul once said, "But may it never be that I should boast, except in the cross of our Lord Jesus Christ, through which the world has been crucified to me, and I to the world." (Galatians 5:14) It is the Cross of Calvary alone which crucifies the love of the world in the human heart.

THE WHORE OF BABYLON

The spirit that is attacking and tempting the Church today is merely the modern face of something very ancient. "Babylon the Great" is the term used in the Book of Revelation to name the spirit of *kosmos*, this seducing spirit that offers people a life outside of God and His rule. Throughout this book I have attempted to express some of the ways this spirit is at work in our lives, trying to lead us away from our dependence on God.

But there is a second personality unveiled in John's great vision. It is called the Whore of Babylon. It must be remembered that idolatry and adultery are terms very closely connected in God's mind. He has a people who He considers to be His wife. In O.T. times this was the nation of Israel, but this concept now refers to the Bride of Christ—the Christian Church. An adulteress is a bride who has been unfaithful to her husband. The Whore of Babylon is the unfaithful part of the Church which is sleeping with the enemy. "The whore is the apostate Church, just as *the woman* (ch. 12) is *the Church while faithful*," says the commentary of Jamieson, Fausset, Brown (c. 1870). "[It comprises] the whole apostate Church, Roman, Greek, and even Protestant, so far as it has been seduced from its 'first love' (ch. 2:4) to Christ, the heavenly Bridegroom, and given its affections to worldly pomps and idols."[3]

Also written over a hundred years ago, way back before the modern deception began asserting itself (when men's minds weren't so clouded by the insidious influences of the spirit of Antichrist), the *Pulpit Commentary* contains the following observations about the Whore of Babylon:

Note the remarkable similarity between these words and those of chap. 21:9, and the contrast between the bride, the wife of the Lamb, and the harlot who is connected with the beast.... There seems to be no doubt that this figure describes the degenerate portion of the Church of God. (1) As we have already seen, this symbolism is made use of by St. John to portray the faithlessness of those who are professedly servants of God....

Wherever professedly Christian men have thought the world's favor better than its reproach; wherever they have esteemed its honors a more desirable possession than its shame; wherever they have courted ease rather than welcomed suffering, have loved self-indulgence rather than self-sacrifice, and have substituted covetousness in grasping for generosity in distributing what they had—there the spirit of Babylon has been manifested....

The harlot is Babylon; that is, that the worldly portion of the Church, though nominally Christian, is in reality identical with the world, which is openly antagonistic to God. This faithless (though outwardly Christian) portion of Christ's Church is the mother, that is, the cause of the existence of unfaithfulness to God. So true is it that the professing Christian who is worldly minded does more to cause in others disobedience and unfaithfulness to God, than he who openly declares himself in opposition to God....

(Verse 2), therefore, declares that this faithless portion of the Church has chosen rather to render to the world that love which is due to God, and to be connected rather with the powers of this world than to have its treasure in heaven.[4]

THE GREAT APOSTASY

By the time this age comes to a close, a major part of Christendom will be in league with the spirit of Antichrist. In the passage of Scripture where Paul warned about the powerful nature of the deception which would accompany the Antichrist, he also said that our "gathering together to" Jesus would not occur "unless the apostasy comes first." (2 Thessalonians 2:3) He used a different form of the same Greek word in 1 Timothy 4 when he says, "the Spirit explicitly says that in later times some will fall away from the faith." Jesus also mentioned this apostasy as one of the characteristics of the spiritual atmosphere of those days prior to His return when He said, "Many will fall away." (Matthew 24:10)

What is this apostasy? *Strong's Bible Dictionary* defines the Greek *apostasia* as a "defection from truth... falling away, forsake."[5] The *International Standard Bible Encyclopedia* goes into a little more depth: "a standing away from, a falling away, a withdrawal, a defection... abandonment of the faith."[6] The *Vine's Word Dictionary* says, "a defection, revolt... to forsake... used politically of rebels."[7]

There are two things which stand out from these definitions. First, the word means a forsaking of something a person once had; in regards to religious beliefs, it would constitute the abandonment of a relationship with God once held. This word does not indicate, as some teach, that he is referring to some of the mainline denominations that have become coldly religious. He is talking about people not organizations. These are evangelicals who have abandoned their relationship with the Lord. In the inner man—that secret part of us that only God sees—they have forsaken the Lord. Because they still maintain an outward façade of Christianity, they will eventually be assigned "a place with the hypocrites; weeping shall be there and the gnashing of teeth." (Matthew 24:51)

Secondly, it is interesting that this Greek word can be used not only to describe those who forsake religious beliefs, but also applies to those who rebel against authority. The spirit of Antichrist is the one who develops and encourages rebellion against God's authority on this earth. It certainly stands to reason that he would be at work in the hearts and minds of believers as well. We are all rebellious by nature, and the devil loves to cultivate that natural tendency in Christians.

We have already seen how a great apostasy has been predicted. The river of delusion is rising. The whole world is being swept toward the giant waterfall that will spill its inhabitants into the lake of fire. It is the broad way. It is the way of *kosmos*. Jesus was careful to show His people the way of escape. In His discourse on the last days, He repeatedly warned His followers to be READY, to be ALERT, to be AWAKE! The warning is there, it is up to us to heed it.

"An unwatchful church will soon become an unholy church.... The main cure of a church comes by strengthening its inner life. When we live near to Jesus, when we drink from the fountain-head of eternal truth and purity, when we become personally true and pure, then our watchfulness is, under God, our safeguard, and heresy, false doctrine, and unclean profession are kept far away. Sleeping guards invite the enemy. He who leaves his door unlocked asks the thief to enter. Watchfulness is always profitable, and slothfulness is always dangerous."[1]

-C.H. Spurgeon

14

READY FOR THE LORD

The second coming of Jesus Christ will be the most momentous event on planet earth since Calvary. Holy saints have patiently awaited His return for nearly 2,000 years. Can you imagine what His presence will mean to this earth?

At various periods of world history, the signs of the times seemed to point to His return, but one question was always difficult to answer, namely: how would the Antichrist gain control over the economies of the world so completely that no one could buy or sell without his name, number or mark? Today's generation knows the answer, of course — the modern high-speed computer makes it possible.

The Japanese are currently building a supercomputer capable of producing 130 quadrillion* calculations per second. One can only imagine the computing capacity the global government will have access to once the Antichrist takes

---

* A quadrillion is a cardinal number followed by 15 zeroes, or 1,000 trillion.

control of the world's population. In Sweden, a corporation called Epicenter is already inserting microchips which function as swipe cards into workers' hands. The globalist movement has successfully brought mankind right to the threshold of a one-world government.

In these perilous times, is the Church standing ready, spiritually alert and sober? Are saints redeeming their time in anticipation of standing before God? Are they living to please God alone—their commitment reinforced by the signs of the times? Tragically, the answer seems negative. A majority of those who claim to be followers of Christ are actually far more concerned about who will win the next Super Bowl or be the next president. Many think that watching for the Second Coming equates with reading action-packed novels about the Tribulation and watching movies about those who remain on earth after the "rapture." They don't realize that the spirit of Babylon has successfully turned "watching" into Christian entertainment. The very thing that should prepare their hearts for Christ's return is intoxicating them out of the needed spiritual sobriety! Others presume they are prepared because they study end-time charts and graphs, when the truth is that a superficial knowledge of prophecy does nothing to prepare one for it.

THE HOUR OF TEMPTATION

Two major themes appear in Jesus' last days discourse found in Matthew 24 and 25 (and reinforced in Luke 21). The first theme—found in Matthew 24:1-41—is an overview of physical and spiritual signs that will mark the end of the age with a recurrent warning against deception. The second theme, which is what concerns us in this chapter, begins with verse 42 and runs to the end of chapter 25. It is an urgent warning to be *ready*, and is supported by several parables, which describe not only how important readiness will be, but also *how* to be ready.

Jesus saw the terrible battle ahead for His followers when all the principalities and powers of evil would be arrayed against them before His return. He saw a time when Satan and his angels would do everything possible to distract, seduce and wear out God's people in order to keep them from a true desire for His return. "Therefore be on the alert," He taught, "for you do not know which day your Lord is coming.... For this reason you be ready too; for the Son of Man is coming at an hour when you do not think He will." (Matthew 24:42, 44) This warning was followed by two supporting parables: The Wise and Foolish Servants (Matthew 24:45-51) and The Ten Virgins (*Matthew 25:1-13*). This last parable concludes with the words, "Be on the alert then, for you do not know the day nor the hour."

Jesus was very concerned about the spiritual attentiveness of His people at the end of the Age.

To get a sense of this urgent warning, we can go back to the warnings Jesus gave His disciples at a time when the devil's power was unleashed against Him nearly two thousand years ago in the Garden of Gethsemane. In a way, the events of that night foreshadow what believers can expect at the end of this age.

> Then Jesus came with them to a place called Gethsemane, and said to His disciples, "Sit here while I go over there and pray." And He took with Him Peter and the two sons of Zebedee, and began to be grieved and distressed. Then He said to them, "My soul is deeply grieved, to the point of death; remain here and keep watch with Me." And He went a little beyond them, and fell on His face and prayed, saying, "My Father, if it is possible, let this cup pass from Me; yet not as I will, but as Thou wilt."
>
> And He came to the disciples and found them sleeping, and said to Peter, "So, you men could not keep watch with Me for one hour? Keep watching and praying, that you may

not enter into temptation; the spirit is willing, but the flesh is weak." He went away again a second time and prayed, saying, "My Father, if this cannot pass away unless I drink it, Thy will be done."

And again He came and found them sleeping, for their eyes were heavy. And He left them again, and went away and prayed a third time, saying the same thing once more. Then He came to the disciples, and said to them, "Are you still sleeping and taking your rest? Behold, the hour is at hand and the Son of Man is being betrayed into the hands of sinners." (Matthew 26:36-45)

From this sobering account, we can draw some meaningful inferences for our own situation.

First, we see that *Jesus gave His disciples very clear instructions.* His sense of urgency was unmistakable: "My soul is deeply grieved, to the point of death; remain here and keep watch with Me." In the three-and-a-half years they had followed Jesus, they had never seen Him in such a state of anguish. He had told them more than once that He would be arrested and crucified, but now He was "grieved to the point of death." This was a pivotal moment in the history of the world because the conflict that was going on over Jesus Christ was a life and death battle for the human race. His words were *urgent.* Now was not the time to fall asleep!

The Master, who was typically calm and peaceful, was so agitated that He asked for help in prayer, especially from Peter, James and John. What an opportunity for them to support Him! He sought their prayers in His darkest hours on earth. This was holy ground. From a stone's throw away they could see Him agonizing in prayer. Probably they could hear Him crying out to the Father. Yet, at such a critical time, they were overwhelmed by the powers of darkness and fell asleep. How could it be?

It is interesting that when He approached the three sleeping disciples, His words were directed to Peter. This was the same man who a couple of hours earlier had boldly exclaimed, "Lord, with You I am ready to go both to prison and to death!" (Luke 22:33) "I will lay down my life for You," he had confidently asserted. (John 13:37) Peter had an extremely exaggerated idea of his readiness to face what was coming. *Unfortunately, most believers today have this same cocky attitude!*

The disciples were confident, but there was something they did not understand. "Keep watching and praying, that you may not enter into temptation," Jesus had told them, because "the spirit is willing, but the flesh is weak." Did they take it in? Did they really know that their flesh was weak? Their lofty intentions withered under the spiritual attack they encountered that night.[†]

Many Christians today are making the same mistake the disciples made. They firmly believe that they are ready. They sing about it. They teach about it. They even boast about it. Instead of the sobriety one would expect concerning such matters, there is a flippancy that is almost astounding. Solomon said, "The prudent sees the evil and hides himself, but the naïve go on, and are punished for it." (Proverbs 22:3) Brimming with confidence, churchgoers are striding toward the coming of the Lord almost without a care in the world. However, many of them are so *intoxicated with Babylon* that they cannot comprehend the spiritual realities happening around them. *They are out of it!*

Sleeping

Repeatedly, Jesus uses the same word in regard to His Coming that He used with His disciples that fateful night in

---

† It should be noted that the disciples couldn't stay awake. They did not have access to the power of God to resist the enemy at that point. However, after Calvary, a tremendous spiritual power was released for believers that enables us to stand in the face of temptation. It should also be noted that the disciples did wake up after Calvary and, in turn, woke up the entire world!

Gethsemane. What word is that? "WATCH!" Nevertheless, as a collective body of disciples, we are drowsy and lethargic and our spiritual eyelids are heavy with sleep. Jesus is calling to us, "Watch! Stay alert! Wake up!"

How can we be so spiritually drowsy when we are heading into mankind's most urgent hour? Where is our zeal for God? Why is it that we can work ourselves to the point of exhaustion on our jobs but are so sluggish when it comes to helping the hungry, the homeless or those in prison? Why is it that we can watch television by the hour but are too tired to read the Word of God? Why are saints so acutely aware of every little "hurt" from others but unmoved by the reality that our neighbors are slipping into hell? Why aren't we Christians trembling in fear of the Christ who gave His life to save us? Is it because we are sound asleep? Could it be that we are being "worn down" by the spirit of Antichrist? (Daniel 7:25) Is it possible that our supposed peace with God is simply the dulled senses of someone under the spell of satanic enchantment?

The fact is, nothing dulls one's spiritual sensitivity like *kosmos*. Even believers with the best of intentions find that their passion for God wanes in the polluted atmosphere of Babylon. Nothing deadens a love for the Father like "the things in the world." It is interesting how wide awake we are when it comes to our life in Babylon. When it comes to Mammon, we rise early and stay up late. Our undivided attention is given to sports scores, blockbuster movies, late-night TV, political trivia and the latest Hollywood gossip.

Right now the Church is like Samson, sleeping peacefully in the lap of Delilah, not hearing the snip of the scissors, not knowing that the God-given strength in its body is draining away by the minute. The voice of *kosmos* sings pleasing lullabies, and her caresses have completed the seduction. I can assure you that Satan and his "Philistine" henchmen are wide awake, standing just outside the door as we slumber, cradled in the arms of the seducer.

It's no wonder that Jesus asked, "When the Son of Man comes, will He find faith on the earth?" (Luke 18:8b) Jesus looked for those who would watch for Him in Gethsemane, and He is looking for those who will be faithful watchers now. This time they MUST stay awake. There must be proof that the devil's incessant taunts to Jesus are false, when he says, "You can't get anyone to care about Your return. Look at them! They live for what I give them, not for what You offer. They'll ALL BE ASLEEP when You return!"

READY FOR THE COMING OF THE LORD

As we draw closer to the return of Christ, the battle between good and evil (light and darkness) will intensify. The temptation to feast at the devil's banquet table will increase, and many will succumb to spiritual sluggishness as they gorge themselves on the devil's delicacies.

Christians must learn NOW how to say "NO!" to this world's system if they intend to withstand the great shaking that is fast approaching. Jesus told the disciples, "Keep watching and praying, that you may not enter into temptation; the spirit is willing, but the flesh is weak." (Matthew 26:41)

It is vital that we as believers acknowledge that our flesh is weak and that, most likely, we are not nearly as prepared for the coming conflict as we think. Unless we humble ourselves and agree with Jesus about the seriousness of our present condition, we will never seek the help we need. Jesus said, "It is not those who [think they] are healthy who need a physician, but those who are sick. But go and learn what this means, 'I desire mercy, and not sacrifice,' for I did not come to call the [self] righteous, but sinners to repentance." (Matthew 9:12-13) *The Pharisee never sees how sick he is.* His pride throws up walls to block out Jesus' diagnosis of his condition. Do you really know, dear one, just how weak your flesh is?

It is also vital that we "watch and pray." Jesus used the word "watch" many times in His discourses on the last days in Matthew 24, Mark 13, and Luke 21. Paul and Peter issued the same command in their epistles, calling for spiritual sober-mindedness and alertness. There are two aspects to "watching" that need to be considered. The first aspect doesn't need much explanation; it is the natural meaning we ascribe to the words alert and sober. Paul wrote, "Let us not sleep as others do, but let us be alert and sober." (1 Thessalonians 5:6) He also said, "Be on the alert, stand firm in the faith, act like men, be strong." (1 Corinthians 16:13) Peter said, "Be of sober spirit, be on the alert. Your adversary, the devil, prowls about like a roaring lion, seeking someone to devour." (1 Peter 5:8)

Perhaps the most accurate picture of this concept would be the military sentry. In Vietnam, soldiers on guard duty knew that they were facing a relentless enemy who would take any opportunity to overrun the camp. The safety of their fellow soldiers depended entirely upon their ability to remain wide awake throughout the night and especially right before dawn, when sleep seemed most irresistible and the enemy was most likely to attack.

Jesus' parable of the householder waiting for his lord's return (Matthew 24:42-45) underscores this meaning of wakefulness; so does the Parable of the Wise and Foolish Virgins. The application is so clear—we have to remain alert, sober and watchful even into the darkest hours of the night.

However, there is more involved in the meaning of the word "watch" than being alert and sober. A deeper meaning of the word is expressed in the other end-time parables found in Matthew 24 and 25. It has to do with *the quality of a person's spiritual life.*

THE WISE AND FOOLISH SERVANTS

The parable of the two servants gives us this fuller understanding of what it means to watch:

> "Who then is the faithful and sensible slave whom his master put in charge of his household to give them their food at the proper time? Blessed is that slave whom his master finds so doing when he comes. Truly I say to you, that he will put him in charge of all his possessions.
>
> "But if that evil slave says in his heart, 'My master is not coming for a long time,' and shall begin to beat his fellow slaves and eat and drink with drunkards; the master of that slave will come on a day when he does not expect him and at an hour which he does not know, and shall cut him in pieces and assign him a place with the hypocrites; weeping shall be there and the gnashing of teeth." (Matthew 24:45-51)

Jesus paints a sharp contrast between these two slaves of His. The first servant is labeled "blessed" because he is feeding his master's other servants when the master returns. If the master appears suddenly in the dead of night, this servant has nothing to fear. He is simply busy doing what he has been instructed to do. When the Master appears, this servant will "have confidence and not shrink away from Him in shame at His coming." (1 John 2:28) Like the Thessalonians, he knows the seriousness of being ready. "For you yourselves know full well that the day of the Lord will come just like a thief in the night. While they are saying, 'Peace and safety!' then destruction will come upon them suddenly like birth pangs upon a woman with child; and they shall not escape." (1 Thessalonians 5:2-3)

Jesus calls the second servant "evil," because he had no concern for the needs of those in his charge, nor was he concerned that the master might return at any hour. Peter describes that kind of attitude that doesn't care: "Know this first of all, that in the last days mockers will come with their mocking, *following after their own lusts*, and saying, 'Where is the promise of His coming? For ever since the fathers fell asleep, all continues just as it was from the beginning of creation.'" (2 Peter 3:3-4) What "lusts"? "The lust of the flesh and the lust of the eyes and the boastful pride of life." (1 John 2:16) The deeply buried attitude is, "All is well; there is nothing to be concerned about."

The "evil" servant is also beating his fellow slaves, not physically, of course, but *inwardly*. Jesus is referring to the attitude of his heart. This person is hard on others, critical and judgmental. Perhaps he is bitter toward those who have crossed his will or resents those who have offended him. If he ever had any true love for others it has long since grown cold. (Matthew 24:12)

Jesus also said that this "evil" servant is "eating" when his Master returns. This represents living in selfish indulgence. Like those in the days of Noah, he is eating, drinking, buying, selling, and building. (Luke 17:26-28) In short, this person is living for SELF and for temporal satisfaction. He has very little time for and devotion to other people.

Last, he is found "drinking" with drunkards. Drunkenness characterizes those who are out of touch with reality. He is so inebriated with the spirit of the world that he does not have a clue as to what is going on around him or what is his purpose in life. *He is out of it!*

What lies ahead for the "evil" servant, who refuses to prepare himself for his lord's return? Jesus said that he is sent to a special place reserved in hell for those who live the outward façade of Christianity without an inward life with God. His lord "shall cut him in pieces and assign him a place with the hypocrites; weeping shall be there and the gnashing of teeth." (Matthew 24:51)

The two-fold truth expressed in this parable is then reinforced in the three parables of Matthew 25. The story of the Wise and Foolish Virgins repeats the warning: "Be on the alert then, for you do not know the day nor the hour." (Matthew 25:13) The parables of the Talents and the Sheep and Goats (Matthew 25:14-30; 31-46) both emphasize the fact that living out God's love to others is one of the most important factors to being in a state of readiness to meet God. Dear one, what is the Spirit saying to you?

CLAMMERING TO AND FRO

One more important element of remaining spiritually alert that I must touch upon is referred to in Luke's rendition of the Lord's discourse about the last days. Jesus said, "Be on guard, so that your hearts will not be weighted down with dissipation and drunkenness and the worries of life, and that day will not come on you suddenly like a trap." (Luke 21:34) In secular literature, this word "dissipation" describes the lingering after-effects of a night out on the town. The man has a hangover; he is sickly, worn out and lethargic. In the context of a person's spiritual life, dissipation refers to the dullness of heart and spiritual barrenness that results from a life full of worldly activities.

Certainly, our post-modern world can accurately be described with the word motion. We are living in a time of unprecedented activity. People are rushing, people are moving, people are "on the go," living their lives in ceaseless locomotion. Stand on any bustling street corner and witness the stress that is etched into people's faces. Lean over a freeway overpass and watch the endless rush of speeding cars, often driven by frustrated and even angry drivers. Park near an airport and observe the crowded planes bound for multiple worldwide destinations. Truly, the whole world is in a full-court press. Of course, this was foretold in Scripture as one of the overriding characteristics of the end times: "many shall run (Heb. *shut*: rushing around) to and fro, and knowledge shall be increased." (Daniel 12:4 KJV)

Intoxicated with Babylon

Americans have become—dare I say it?—addicted to this fast-paced lifestyle. Indeed, television programming experts now say that in order to hold a viewer's attention, the scene must change on the screen *every three seconds*, or they will become bored and change the channel! How much more will this be the case as entranced young video-gamers become the driving force behind modern society?

One of the unfortunate effects of such frenetic living has been a high level of impatience in people's lives. Our daily decisions are affected, much more than most of us realize, by how quickly we can accomplish a given task. Ray Kroc was among the first to capitalize on this new phenomenon when he opened a chain of "fast food" restaurants named McDonald's™. The enormous success he enjoyed certainly did not come from the quality of the food he offered but from the fact that he could provide it instantly—*without waiting*. In our frenzied tempo of life, we want what we want NOW!

It should go without saying that the flesh thrives in such an environment. Interestingly, the third and fourth "fruits of the Spirit" cited in Galatians 5 are peace and patience (listed ahead of such qualities as kindness, goodness, faithfulness, gentleness, etc.). The writer of Hebrews could not possibly have been more straightforward when he wrote: "Ye have need of patience." (Hebrews 10:36 KJV) Truer words have never been written for today's churchgoer.

Ministers are not exempt from this carnal characteristic either. With over-booked schedules, ringing telephones, piles of mail to sort through, emails to answer, rushing from one appointment to the next, pastors today more closely resemble business entrepreneurs than shepherds of the flock. Imagine the devastating effect this has on their spiritual capacity to lead people into the presence of the Almighty. We would all do well to heed the oft quoted warning of Corrie Ten Boom: "Beware of the barrenness of a busy life."

Truth be told, we have lost the ability (even the desire) to quiet ourselves before God and to truly hear His voice. It was the solitude found in the vast wastelands of the wilderness (a place of excruciating boredom to modern believers) that produced God-filled men like Moses, David and Paul. Even as recently as a hundred years ago, pastors understood what it meant to *sit still* and wait upon God. They learned how to receive divine inspiration for their people through the discipline of tarrying before the Lord.

Unfortunately, most of today's pastors have effectively tuned God out in favor of the roar of Babylon through the media. They no longer have the spiritual sensitivity to hear the Father's still small voice. Rather than subduing their flesh through a daily time of prolonged soaking in God's presence, they hurry through their prayer times (if they even have one), throwing themselves headlong into the day's busy schedule. Instead of receiving a fresh impartation from God that has the power to touch people's hearts, they prepare their sermons by gleaning information from books and presenting it in nicely packaged, three-point messages.

No wonder the Church—with all its programs, building projects, and endless round of activities—produces such meager and superficial fruit. In fact, it seems that the more ministries strive to accomplish, the less they produce anything of eternal value. Rather than waiting to hear the Lord's direction and calmly *getting in the flow of what He is doing*, too often ministry leaders attempt to accomplish their own agendas through their own hard work. To such an attitude the prophet exclaimed, "You have sown much, but harvest little... You look for much, but behold, it comes to little." (Haggai 1:6, 9) The Psalmist wrote, "Unless the LORD builds the house, they labor in vain who build it..." (Psalm 127:1) Jesus said, "...he who abides in Me and I in him, he bears much fruit, for apart from Me you can do nothing." (John 15:5)

I once heard it said that God moves in a great calm. He is the great I AM who dwells outside of the realm of motion and time. Surely one of the keys to being prepared for the return of Christ must be to dwell in His Spirit. Reading end time novels, watching "tribulation" movies, or even studying eschatology do not prepare a person for the Lord's coming. One is prepared by walking in the Spirit, keeping oneself unstained by this world and living out the love of God. "Blessed is that slave whom his master finds so doing when he comes." (Matthew 24:46)

READY FOR THE LORD

"How you have fallen from heaven, O star of the morning, son of the dawn! You have been cut down to the earth, you who have weakened the nations! But you said in your heart, 'I will ascend to heaven; I will raise my throne above the stars of God, and I will sit on the mount of assembly in the recesses of the north. I will ascend above the heights of the clouds; I will make myself like the Most High.' Nevertheless you will be thrust down to Sheol, to the recesses of the pit."[1]

-The Prophet Isaiah to the "king of Babylon"

"Woe, woe, the great city, Babylon, the strong city! For in one hour your judgment has come."[2]

-Lovers of Babylon lamenting over her fall

15

THE FALL OF BABYLON

It was a momentous occurrence in the spiritual realm when the king of Babylon rose up against Jerusalem, the city of God, in 605 B.C. Perhaps hundreds of young Jews were taken captive and herded in chains across the plateaus of Syria to their new home in Mesopotamia. It was an eastward journey of horror for many of God's chosen people.

Once they reached the land of their captors, the Babylonians divided them into groups. Some were allowed to make a life for themselves in Babylon. Some were sent into cruel slavery. But for a group of young men who were set apart for the king's use, life was different. They entered a special three-year training program to serve in the king's palace.

They may have witnessed hundreds of their brethren hauled off in chains as slaves, as we can only imagine the impression such scenes made on their young minds. Surely they faced a strong temptation to please their new masters in every way, for the barbaric cruelty of the Babylonians was well known around the world. The slightest infraction could bring savage punishment. But the fear of physical torture probably influenced these impressionable young Jews far less than the prospect facing them: training for the king's court! Babylon was the greatest nation on earth, and to serve in the king's court was considered the highest privilege. The power emanating from the throne room of Nebuchadnezzar was fearful, intimidating, overwhelming. Who could resist it? It demanded the utmost subservience. Anyone who has been around powerful and influential people understands the pressure to be accepted.

Into this setting were thrown four young Jews named Daniel, Hananiah, Mishael and Azariah. "But Daniel *made up his mind that he would not defile himself* with the king's choice food or with the wine which he drank." (Daniel 1:8) Daniel would do whatever he was told up to a point; but he refused to compromise God's commandments one iota for all the riches of Babylon. That conviction characterized his life in Babylon for the next seventy years.

BELSHAZZAR'S FEAST

Many years passed in the life of Daniel. The kingdom of Babylon saw several rulers come and go. Eventually, Belshazzar, one of Nebuchadnezzar's grandsons became king.

One fateful day, a courier brought to Daniel an invitation from the new king to attend a special banquet. Every important nobleman and dignitary in the land would be there. It would be akin to a White House Dinner Party for the President and his honored guests. Unbeknownst to Belshazzar, it would be his last meal, for at that very moment Darius the Mede had diverted the Euphrates River upstream and was about to bring his Persian army into Babylon through the river gate.

Eating and drinking wine at Belshazzar's Feast is an illustration of living the full life on earth oblivious to the impending judgment. It is the spirit the Jews were in to whom Jesus said, "You seek Me, not because you saw signs, but because you ate of the loaves, and were filled." (John 6:26) It is the same attitude expressed by the wicked slave of Matthew 24 who was eating and drinking with drunkards when his Master returned. It is what Jesus predicted when He said, "And just as it happened in the days of Noah... they were eating, they were drinking, they were marrying, they were being given in marriage, until the day that Noah entered the ark, and the flood came and destroyed them all." (Luke 17:26-27)

Babylon is a picture of living life apart from God. It is a life dominated by self-will, self-sufficiency and self-indulgence. It is also a life that can be very intoxicating and almost irresistible, even for the believer. In our analogy here, the world is in a feast and the spirit of Antichrist is the Babylonian king giving it. Daniel's life is an example to every believer. *He lived in Babylon without being tainted by its spirit or seduced by its glamour.*

Ironically, these same two groups represented in this story can be found throughout the Church world today. The overwhelming majority of professing Christians live day and night for the flesh-gratifying way of life that Babylon offers. They may outwardly call themselves followers of Christ, but their hearts and lifestyles clearly contradict their profession of faith. Paul recognized them in the Church of his day: "For many walk, of whom I often told you, and now tell you even weeping, that they are enemies of the cross of Christ, whose end is destruction, whose god is their appetite, and whose glory is in their shame, who set their minds on earthly things." (Philippians 3:18-19)

The other group is made up of those who choose the narrow path of the Cross and are identified by Jesus as the "chosen few" in Matthew 20:16. They will not be found gorging themselves at the table of the king of Babylon when their Master returns. Instead, they will be ushered into "the marriage supper of the Lamb." Holy living and a love for others will have characterized their lives in Babylon.

The Missing Noble

There was one who was conspicuous by his absence on the night of Belshazzar's feast: Daniel. Whether Belshazzar invited him or not, we don't know; but he wasn't there. Understanding fully the tremendous honor this was and that his failure to appear could cause him to fall out of whatever favor he might have had with the king, Daniel was not interested in attending a self-indulgent feast of the flesh. Maybe he stayed home purposely that night to spend time seeking God. Perhaps he was reading the Scriptures by candlelight, studying the life of Joseph in Potiphar's house. Or maybe he was going over the story of Elijah's confrontations with Ahab and Jezebel.

Daniel was having his own feast, but it was a feast with God. He didn't need their roasted lamb, because he was eating the Bread of Life. He had no taste for their wine, because he was drinking the Living Water. His heart was with God, and he sought for treasures in heaven rather than the spoils of this earth. Mammon had never been his god.

It is interesting that when the handwriting appeared on the wall, the Queen knew whom to call. No one sought the help of compromising Jews who had tried appeasing the king of Babylon. They, like Lot with his sons-in-law, had long since lost their spiritual credibility. The situation called for a man of God, a man who would not compromise or lay aside his godly convictions. When Daniel showed up, immediately the king began offering him everything imaginable. "I'll give you a scarlet robe and I'll put a chain around your neck and I'll make you third in the kingdom," the shaken monarch blubbered on. To this Daniel replied, "Keep your gifts for yourself, or give your rewards to someone else." Daniel was not interested in what the king of Babylon had to offer. He could not be bought.

The world is in a Belshazzar's feast and does not know it. Rubbing elbows with them at the same party are many who name the name of Christ but are both *in* the world and *of* the world! They are deluded as they cheerfully propose one toast after another, becoming more intoxicated with the things of this world by the minute. They are celebrating. Everything is going great. They are like the backslidden minister who frequented a house of prostitution many times without incident. Each time he returned he was less inhibited, and his confidence was strengthened. One night, SUDDENLY, the police raided the place, and he was hauled off to jail with everybody else.

Belshazzar's feast was indeed the gala celebration of the century, until a hand appeared and wrote a message on the wall: "You have been weighed in the balances and found wanting." The partygoers were drunk—completely out of it. They were beyond the point of understanding that this was their last night to party. Like the people of Noah's day, "they did not understand until the flood came and took them all away; so shall the coming of the Son of Man be." (Matthew 24:39) Little did they realize that within moments, the king would be dead, Babylon would fall, and the entire kingdom would be turned upside-down.

Jesus said, "When you see all these things, recognize that He is near, right at the door." (Matthew 24:33) At this point, there is still time to escape.

The Point of Decision

The true believer MUST flee this present darkness. He must extricate himself from its entanglements and cut off every alliance with the enemy. (2 Timothy 2:4) He cannot continue to walk hand-in-hand with those who despise the things of God. He must denounce and repent of everything that pulls him away from Jesus. He must break faith with the natural reasonings of his carnal mind and humbly accept the mind of the Spirit. (Romans 8:7) He must allow the Lord to expose his attempt to serve two masters.

God's grace enables the believer to overcome the pull of the world. (Titus 2:11-14) Its enthralling influences *can* be resisted and conquered. The power of lust *can* be broken. (Galatians 5:16) The righteous can find a place of refuge. (Psalm 46:1-3; Proverbs 18:10) The insidious influence of this world's system can be shattered. (Psalm 119:78) A sincere follower of Christ will flee the world's seductions. The revelation of his adulterous heart *will* drive him to his knees in deep repentance, as he implores God to purge every trace of the love of this world from his heart. (Daniel 12:10)

My dear reader, we have come to the point in man's history where the battle lines are clearly delineated. Neutrality is not an option. "Those who dwell upon the earth" will soon be forced to decide who will be their master. The fulfillment of John's words is upon us: "And the world is passing away, and also its lusts; but the one who does the will of God abides forever." (1 John 2:17) Superficial religion will not survive God's purging fire. Religious activity and spiritual platitudes will only deepen a backslider's delusion. Only through deep repentance and a sincere renunciation of this world's attractions will you be shielded from the powerful influence of the spirit of Babylon and be prepared to meet your Maker. Furthermore, you must live in a keen awareness of God's presence in order to remain immune to the infectious presence of *kosmos*. (1 John 5:4-5) Jesus is the Light of this world, which exposes and dispels all darkness. If you love Him with all your heart, He will make you "more than conqueror" in "the midst of this perverse generation."

Oh dear reader, please hear God's cry! Open your ears to hear what the Spirit of God is saying! This is not simply another doomsday message designed to invoke fear and provoke controversy. The world and its lusts *are* passing away! Babylon is like the *Titanic*, confidently bounding through the night, heading for its fate, while *so-called* followers of Christ are living life to its fullest, unconcerned about the impending danger and unaware that seven warnings have gone up to the captain: "Giant icebergs dead-ahead!" Meanwhile, actual followers of Jesus have heeded the warnings and are heading for the lifeboats. They are ridiculed by world-loving compromisers who feast comfortably at the world's banquet table inside the ship. The revelers may scorn their actions, but these followers of the Lamb hear the Shepherd's voice calling, "Come out of her, my people!"

Full of cynicism and unbelief, churchgoers who haven't tasted real repentance, who have never really been converted, scoff at those who are sitting in the lifeboats with their life jackets on. Their mentality can best be summed up by the words of an actual crewmember of the *Titanic*: "Even God Himself couldn't sink this ship!" They may talk about the fact that Jesus is coming, but they do not really believe it. (2 Peter 3:3-4, 9) If they did, their lives would resemble the wise slave who prepared for his master's return, or the wise virgins who were ready when the call to meet the bridegroom went out. They flirt with the world and still imagine they will go up in the "rapture." What sheer delusion that is!

Fellow Christian, if you haven't sandbagged your life against the floodwaters of deception, you have no idea how bad it will get. You are on a pleasure cruise of worldliness, but you do not realize that the ship you are on is bound for destruction. The Spirit of Antichrist is right now at work, "with all the deception of wickedness for those who perish, because they did not receive the love of the truth so as to be saved." (2 Thessalonians 2:10)

I urge you to open your heart to God. Allow God to put His finger right on the loves of your heart that remain devoted to the attractions of this earth. Let Him expose your deepest lusts. Genuine repentance will set you free and save you from the judgment to come!

INTOXICATED WITH BABYLON

I close with this passionate appeal of the great Scottish clergyman and hymnwriter, Horatius Bonar:

> Ah, yes; the fashion of this world passeth away; and they who have followed that fashion, and identified themselves with that world, will find too late that, in gaining the world, they have lost their souls; that, in filling up time with vanity, they have filled eternity with gloom; that, in snatching at the pleasures of earth, they have lost the joys of heaven, and the glories of the everlasting inheritance. Yes, life is brief, and time is swift; generations come and go; graves open and close each day; old and young vanish out of sight; riches depart, and honors fade...
>
> O man, dying man, dweller on a dying earth, living amid sickbeds and deathbeds, and funerals and graves, surrounded by fallen leaves and faded blossoms, the sport of broken hopes, and fruitless joys, and empty dreams, and fervent longings, and never-healing, never-ending heartaches—O man, dying man, wilt thou still follow vanity and lies; still chase pleasure and gaiety; still sow the wind, and reap the whirlwind? After all that has been told thee of earth's weariness, and pleasure's emptiness; after all that thou thyself hast experienced of the poverty of all things here below; after having been so often disappointed, mocked, and made miserable by that world which thou worshippest; and wilt thou still pursue the lusts of the flesh, and lust of the eye, and the pride of life?
>
> O follower of the world, consider thy ways and ponder thy prospects. Look behind thee, and see the utter emptiness of the past. Look before thee, and make sure of something better and more substantial. Look on the right hand and on the left, and see the weary crowds, seeking rest, and finding none. Look beneath thee, to that eternal fire which is preparing for all that forget God. Look above

thee, and see that bright heaven, with all its unutterable gladness, which thou art so madly despising. Think, too, of thy brief time on earth, lent thee, in God's special love, to accomplish thy preparation for the eternal kingdom. And, when thou considerest these things, rouse thyself from thy dream of pleasure, and rest not till thou hast made good the entrance at the strait gate which leadeth unto life.[3]

Notes

INTRODUCTION

1. Steve Harrison, *The Clash of Kingdoms: Rediscovering Our Role in Earth's Greatest Battle*, (Minneapolis, MN: Ardor Media, 2011) p. 8. Used with permission.
2. C. J. Mahaney, *Worldliness: Resisting the Seduction of a Fallen World*, (Wheaton, IL: Crossway Books, 2008) p. 22.
3. *ibid.*, p. 27.

CHAPTER 1

1. a. Matthew Henry, *3,000 Quotations from the Writings of Matthew Henry*, (Fleming H. Revell Co., 1982) p. 343. b. Matthew Henry, as cited in *Ages Digital Library*, (Rio, WI: Ages Software, 2000).
2. C. J. Mahaney, *Worldliness: Resisting the Seduction of a Fallen World*, p. 16.
3. Gerhard Kittel, *Theological Dictionary of the New Testament*, (Grand Rapids, MI: William B. Eerdman's Publishing Co.) p. 460.
4. H.R. Reynolds, *The Pulpit Commentary*, vol. 17, (McLean, VA: McDonald Publishing Co.) p. 13.
5. Watchman Nee, *Love Not the World*, (Wheaton, IL: Tyndale House Publishers, 1978) pp. 14, 37, 38.
6. David Powlison, *Seeing with New Eyes: Counseling and the Human Condition through the Lens of Scripture*, (Phillipsburg, NJ: P&R, 2003) p. 149.
7. George Watson, *Our Own God*, (Pensacola, FL: Chapel Library Press) p. 22.

CHAPTER 2

1. C. S. Lewis, *The Quotable Lewis*, Wheaton, IL: Tyndale House Publishers, 1989) p. 512.
2. Adam Clarke, *The Bethany Parallel Commentary on the Old Testament*, (Minneapolis, MN: Bethany House Publishers, 1983) p. 38.
3. *ibid.*
4. Alexander Hislop, *The Two Babylons*, (Neptune, NJ: Loizeaux Brothers Publishers, 1916) p. 23.
5. *ibid.*, pp. 24-25.
6. Flavius Josephus, *The Works of Josephus*, vol. 2, (Grand Rapids, MI: Baker Book House, 1974) pp. 79-80.
7. Henry M. Morris, *The Long War Against God*, (Grand Rapids, MI: Baker Book House, 1989) p. 257.
8. *Baker Encyclopedia of the Bible*, vol. 1, edited by Walter A. Elwell, (Grand Rapids, MI: Baker Book House, 1988) p. 1006.
9. See *The Two Babylons*.
10. Rex Andrews, *Meditations in the Revelation*, (Zion IL: The Zion Faith Homes, 1991) p. 75.

CHAPTER 3

1. J. C. Ryle, *Remember Lot's Wife* (Pensacola, FL: Chapel Library Press).
2. Steve Harrison, *The Clash of Kingdoms: Rediscovering Our Role in Earth's Greatest Battle*, p. 16. Used with permission.
3. *ibid.*, p. 17. Used with permission.

CHAPTER 4

1. George Hutcheson, *An Exposition of John*, (Lafayette, IN: Sovereign Grace Publishers, 2001) p. 209.
2. Philip Doddridge, as cited in *On Earth as it is in Heaven*, (Shippensburg, PA: Destiny Image, 1993) p. 100.
3. W. B. Godbey, as cited in *Ages Digital Library* (Rio, WI: Ages Software, 2000).
4. Steve Harrison, *The Clash of Kingdoms: Rediscovering Our Role in Earth's Greatest Battle*, p. 31, 177. Used with permission.
5. Kay Arthur, accessed at https://www.christianquotes.info/search-for-a-quote/#axzz4rFLFLLdz on August 30, 2017.

CHAPTER 5

1. A. W. Tozer, *The Knowledge of the Holy*, (Harper & Row Publishers, 1961) p. 103.
2. Andrew Murray, *The Believer's Secret of Holiness*, (Bethany House Publishers, 1984) p. 14.
3. Leighton Ford, *Topical Encyclopedia of Living Quotations*, (Bethany House Publishers, 1982) p. 109.
4. Bishop Foster, as cited in *Ages Digital Library*, (Rio, WI: Ages Software, 2000).
5. Adam Clarke, as cited in *Ages Digital Library*, (Rio, WI: Ages Software, 2000).
6. Aaron Merritt Hills, as cited in *Ages Digital Library*, (Rio, WI: Ages Software, 2000).
7. *ibid.*
8. J. B. Chapman, as cited in *Ages Digital Library*, (Rio, WI: Ages Software, 2000).
9. Alexander Cruden, as cited in *Holiness: Is it Necessary for Salvation*, by I. C. Herendeen (Pensacola, FL: Chapel Library Press).
10. As cited in *The Best of Vance Havner*, (Old Tappan, NJ: Fleming H. Revell Co., 1969) p. 112.
11. Andrew Murray, *The Believer's Secret of Holiness*, p. 70.
12. *ibid*, pp. 73-74.
13. John Owen, *Owen on Holy Spirit*.
14. J.C. Ryle, *Holiness*.

CHAPTER 6

1. Ravi Zacharias, "Getting To Truth: Who Is Jesus? (And Why Does It Matter?)," from lectures delivered at the Harvard Veritas Forum, (Norcross, GA: Ravi Zecharias International Ministries, 1992) tape 2.
2. Steve Harrison, *The Clash of Kingdoms: Rediscovering Our Role in Earth's Greatest Battle*, p. 22. Used with permission.
3. Leonard Ravenhill, as cited in *Holy Fire*, by Michael Brown, (Destiny Image Publishers, 1996) p. 264.
4. Watchman Nee, as cited in *Holy Fire*.
5. Rex Andrews, *Mediations in the Revelation*, p. 92.

CHAPTER 7

1. Richard Baxter, as cited in *On Earth as it is in Heaven*, (Shippensburg, PA: Destiny Image, 1993) p.4.
2. C.H. Spurgeon, as cited in *Ages Digital Library*, (Rio, WI: Ages Software, 2000).

NOTES

3. Matthew Henry, *Commentary on the Whole Bible*, Galatians to Revelation, as cited in *Ages Digital Library*, (Rio, WI: Ages Software, 2000), pp. 766-767.
4. Dietrich Bonhoeffer, *The Cost of Discipleship*, (New York: Collier Books, 1949) pp. 45-47.

CHAPTER 8
1. A.W. Tozer, *The Best of A. W. Tozer*, (Grand Rapids, MI: Baker Book House, 1978) pp. 76, 186.
2. Lev Navrozov, *Inspiring Quotations*, (Nashville, TN: Thomas Nelson Publishers, 1988) p. 57.
3. K.P. Yohannan, *The Road To Reality*, (Creation House, 1988) pp. 73-74.

CHAPTER 9
1. Oswald Chambers, *Oswald Chambers: The Best From All His Books*, (Nashville, TN: Thomas Nelson Publishers, 1987) p. 228.
2. Charles H. Mackintosh, as cited in *On Earth as it is in Heaven*, (Shippensburg, PA: Destiny Image, 1993) p. 104.
3. John MacArthur, Jr., *Our Sufficiency in Christ*, Dallas, TX: Word Publishing, 1991) pp. 58-59.
4. Dave Hunt, *Beyond Seduction*, Eugene, OR: Harvest House Publishers, 1989) p. 111.
5. *Christianity Today International/Today's Christian Woman*, (September-October, 2003).
6. Jay E. Adams, *More Than Redemption*, (Zondervan Publishing, 1979) p. 8.
7. Dave Hunt, *Beyond Seduction*, p. 114.

CHAPTER 10
1. William Gurnall, as cited in *On Earth as it is in Heaven*, (Shippensburg, PA: Destiny Image, 1993) p. 111.
2. Paul Billheimer, *Destined to Overcome: The Technique of Spiritual Warfare*, (Bloomington, MN: Bethany House Publishers, 1982) p. 71.
3. George Verwer, as cited in "Reach the World for Christ at All Costs" *Herald of His Coming*, (February, 2013) accessed at http://www.heraldofhiscoming.com/Past%20Issues/2013/February/herald_international.htm on September 2, 2017.
4. A.W. Tozer, *The Best of A. W. Tozer*, pp. 126-127.
5. Carol Gentry, "Slaves to the set: U.S. hooked on TV" *St. Petersburg Times*, (1996).
6. Don Wildmon, *The Home Invaders*, (Wheaton, IL: Victor Books, 1971) pp. 45-46.
7. A.W. Tozer, *The Best of A. W. Tozer*, pp. 85-86.
8. *Webster's New Collegiate Dictionary*, Springfield, MA: G. & C. Merriam Co., 1960) p. 615.
9. The late Rev. John Woodward, *The Devil's Vision*.

CHAPTER 11
1. Matthew Henry, as cited in *On Earth as it is in Heaven*, (Shippensburg, PA: Destiny Image, 1993) p. 57.
2. Charles H. Spurgeon, as cited in *On Earth as it is in Heaven*, (Shippensburg, PA: Destiny Image, 1993) p. 81.

3. Henry Drummond, as cited in *On Earth as it is in Heaven*, (Shippensburg, PA: Destiny Image, 1993) p. 86.
4. Much of the information about consumerism in this chapter came from the following excellent article, written by Rodney Clapp: "Why The Devil Takes VISA" *Christianity Today*, (October 7, 1996) p. 24.
5. *ibid*, p. 24.
6. *ibid*, p. 27.
7. *ibid*, p. 20.
8. Dave Harvey, "God, My Heart, and Stuff," as cited in *Worldliness: Resisting the Seduction of a Fallen World*, by C. J. Mahaney, (Wheaton, IL: Crossway Books, 2008) pp. 93, 95.
9. *ibid*.
10. John Wesley, as cited in *Ages Digital Library*, (Rio, WI: Ages Software, 2000).
11. Dwight Moody, as cited in *Ages Digital Library*, (Rio, WI: Ages Software, 2000).

CHAPTER 12
1. Oswald Chambers, *Oswald Chambers: The Best From All His Books*, p. 279.
2. A.W. Tozer, *The Knowledge of the Holy*, (New York: Harper and Row Publishers, 1961).
3. W.E. Vine, *Vine's Expository Dictionary of Old and New Testament Words*, vol. 3, (Old Tappan, NJ: Fleming H. Revell Co., 1981) p. 317.

CHAPTER 13
1. Steve Harrison, *The Clash of Kingdoms: Rediscovering Our Role in Earth's Greatest Battle*, p. 34. Used with permission.
2. Matthew Henry, *3,000 Quotations from the Writings of Matthew Henry*, p. 295.
3. Robert Jamieson, Andrew Fausset and David Brown, *The Bethany Parallel Commentary on the New Testament*, (Minneapolis, MN: Bethany House Publishers, 1983) pp. 1481-1482.
4. D. Thomas, *The Pulpit Commentary*, vol. 22, *The Book of Revelation*, p. 427.
5. *Strong's Bible Dictionary*, as cited in *Quick Verse Computer Bible Program*.
6. *International Standard Bible Encyclopedia*, as cited in *Ages Digital Library*, (Rio, WI: Ages Software, 2000).
7. W.E. Vine, *Vine's Expository Dictionary*, p. 73.

CHAPTER 14
1. Charles Spurgeon, as cited in *Ages Digital Library*, (Rio, WI: Ages Software, 2000).

CHAPTER 15
1. Isaiah 14:12-15.
2. Revelation 18:10.
3. Horatius Bonar, *Christ and the World*, (Pensacola, FL: Chapel Library Press).

SECTION QUOTES
All these quotes come from the same source: Leonard Ravenhill, editor, *The Refiner's Fire: A Journal for Those Who Seek a Fuller Revelation of the Lord Jesus Christ*, vol. 1, p. 69.

THE OVERCOMERS SERIES

YOU'VE HAD YOUR BREAKTHROUGH—NOW IT'S TIME TO LIVE IT.

It takes more than a single experience to live the victorious Christian life.
It takes a pattern of godly living.

$60

Why settle for lukewarm Christianity—with its frequent lapses into shameful behavior—when it is possible to enjoy an upright and godly life?

This powerful series will not only teach you how to lead a godly life but will impart to you the very power to do so.

IN THE BOX:

- 12 DVDs featuring 24 specially-chosen messages
- Bonus Features: documentaries, testimonies, interviews, etc.
- Retails at $69.99!

THIS SERIES COVERS:

- Living for Jesus in a Dark World
- What it Means to Follow Jesus
- In Search of Truth
- Living at the Cross
- Leading a Controlled Life in a Lust-Driven Culture
- A Passion to Seek God
- Resisting the Great Lie
- The Set-Apart Life
- For the Love of Pleasure
- Finding Answers for Life's Struggles
- The Self-Life or the Mercy-Life
- The Lordship of Christ

BUY NOW AT STORE.PURELIFEMINISTRIES.ORG

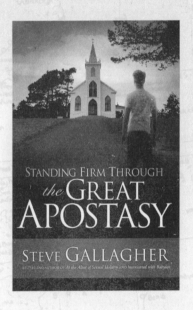

OTHER BOOKS AVAILABLE BY PURE LIFE MINISTRIES

At the Altar of Sexual Idolatry
At the Altar of Sexual Idolatry DVD Curriculum
At the Altar of Sexual Idolatry Workbook
A Biblical Guide to Counseling the Sexual Addict
Create in Me a Pure Heart
Entering His Courts
From Ashes to Beauty
He Leads Me Beside Still Waters
How America Lost Her Innocence
i: the root of sin exposed
A Lamp Unto My Feet
Living in Victory
Out of the Depths of Sexual Sin
Pressing on Toward the Heavenly Calling
Selah! The Book of Psalms in the Richest Translations
Standing Firm through the Great Apostasy
The Overcomers Series (12-DVD set)
The Time of Your Life in Light of Eternity
The Walk of Repentance
When His Secret Sin Breaks Your Heart
Wisdom: Proverbs & Ecclesiastes in the Richest Translations
The Word of Their Testimony

Pure Life Ministries helps Christian men achieve lasting freedom from sexual sin. The Apostle Paul said, "Walk in the Spirit and you will not fulfill the lust of the flesh." Since 1986, Pure Life Ministries (PLM) has been discipling men into the holiness and purity of heart that comes from a Spirit-controlled life. At the root, illicit sexual behavior is sin and must be treated with spiritual remedies. Our counseling programs and teaching resources are rooted in the biblical principles that, when applied to the believer's daily life, will lead him out of bondage and into freedom in Christ.

BIBLICAL TEACHING RESOURCES

Pure Life Ministries offers a full line of books, audio CDs and DVDs specifically designed to give men the tools they need to live in sexual purity.

RESIDENTIAL CARE

The most intense and involved counseling PLM offers comes through the **Residential Program** (9 months), in Dry Ridge, Kentucky. The godly and sober atmosphere on our 45-acre campus provokes the hunger for God and deep repentance that destroys the hold of sin in men's lives.

HELP AT HOME

The **Overcomers At-Home Program** (OCAH) is available for those who cannot come to Kentucky for the Residential Program. This twelve-week counseling program features weekly counseling sessions and many of the same teachings offered in the Residential Program.

CARE FOR WIVES

Pure Life Ministries also offers help to wives of men in sexual sin through our 12-week **At-Home Program for Wives**. Our wives' counselors have suffered through the trials and storms of such a discovery and can offer a devastated wife a sympathetic ear and the biblical solutions that worked in their lives.

PURE LIFE MINISTRIES
14 School St. • Dry Ridge • KY • 41035
Office: 859.824.4444 • Orders: 888.293.8714
inform@purelifeministries.org
www.purelifeministries.org